SPLASH BREEZE
THE ANGEL POINT PATH
DESTINY COLLECTION

500 AFFIRMED PHILOSOPHY GOALS AND
SKILLLS MANAGEMENT TOOL BOOK

CORY MORR

authorHOUSE®

AuthorHouse™
1663 Liberty Drive
Bloomington, IN 47403
www.authorhouse.com
Phone: 1 (800) 839-8640

Published by AuthorHouse 12/23/2016

ISBN: 978-1-5246-5606-5 (sc)
ISBN: 978-1-5246-5605-8 (e)

Library of Congress Control Number: 2016921120

Print information available on the last page.

CHRISTILISM

The miracle Epiphany of master Jesus Christ and chosen Lord savior contrasts a forced religious congreration to appease unchanged custom of taboo for anyone, or to a mortal's independence of opinion. A member's honesty of charity benefits begotten devition and worth for praising the temple Zion heaven chambers unnamed reserved ownership is an unprecedented identity standing on Montain Cities before the statues of the King. The grace in front before the Holy church of which what elusive is your initial father, provides validity to persuade detachment of an erroneous plague appaling habit; otherwise, assessable presumption miscontrue foreshadowed distinction of that modest perfection. Restore purity untouched should always avow support of outstanding serviced work saved through healed thanksgiving altogether.

Before daily problems align commitment for self-revealing yourselves, rebuilding a membered foundation of relative improved qualities, place a fond dedication of redemption than suffering chance to reshape alternative change. Practicing endurance to leap dragged obstacles dropped overhead such inner beyond-power. Reject unconditional hurtful crucifixion, deploying than disposing impeccable talents you protest objective curiosity to risk intrigue. Riddle exquisite features for uncovering demonstrated magic ascendable for the decedents of the selective righteous orphans fostering holy-angelic interstellar enchantment for immortal structure and sensible direction of named authority angelic humans plot escapable termination for a prevention lead purposeful balance themselves order to regulate harmony.

"Born is the millenium covenant of the Christilities."

144,000   -Cory Morr

1. Apply outreached gain of variances obtained possessions courteous grandeur effort relieves an irritated bump of the pavement; investment of materialism configures stretched assailed work criticizes clement profits beyond and lucrative retrieved resources typically induces bacterial remission sprains secure, near submerged swim a float a lake until a sudden waddled swan quacks a shore; currents feathered swarm sworn claws prevailed saintly fathers assembled abided seas cometh among trees from these heard noisy uproars.

2. If a stone was thrown into a pond, but it was the last stone previous to the other bigger rocks, would that pebble be also thrown ever? Nevertheless, kissed on its brow the sun of a horizon kingdom? Though the tiniest bread speaks multitudes of flying doves vacating passible migrant travel, it also illustrates the dawn of an instructing river, a stream of thoughts traveling shameless bravery, and divest admonition in the intricate atoll-less-rants evaporating immune truth the missing flawed point would divert a hardheaded disorder down underneath the soft-spoken ravine, floated tall to the ceiling tops.

3. Fearless valor is non-negotiable, a tag cannot be discounted a priceless prince of immeasurable weighted program of rewarded problems floated over a day, no year curtailed uncertain indefinite hours per week. No bargain can be unreached unsettled kosher disloyal, because courage by layaway coincidence usually begins through the first procedure case self-signifying "I contemplated about my plans" and 2nd "I've judged my criteria trends and outlooks and going to assess that persuaded sample," last "I've heard and seen the fact this idea is a great solution; I've indicated the possible reasonable offer you have provided me and sufficed my determined approached option methods facilitated easily."

4. The sooner the wicked deceitful confess their misjudged sins, a cup of salvationwill anoint their lips bathed from a blossomed orchard falling petals of a real LOVE elder's kiss with quelled forgiveness.

5. An oasis wastes natural resources to save a disheveled disciple, while a mirage blinds the fools arresting mourning wells of their faces, left the children hungry whimpering their shadows stained of broken bones, and shadows of dried unattended injures uncovered empty.

6. A tree is only unlearned if it has no garden enriched nutrients mothered to bear parenting LOVE; then, how much extra wisdom will that room capture the teacher's catch of the storm, before it is edified in a chair, but of a constructed church? A temple opens authority of the mouth of golden gates and elders for books through most a heritage establishes significance.

7. If an apples applies raw terror of discipled law of hope and faith of now statues revised in the closed windows or of the thunderous world, the fruit's harmony to flourish the vineyard's crop will dispatch un-given serenity to the unthinkable non-empathizers.

8. Time waits impatiently for no one, it's hot air of missing what you did not do yesterday, and what you regret expectation of irresolute uncertainty you could not afford early, or before today an organized convenience consequent placed is met.

9. Time bakes meadows, as flexibility grows demonstrating the majority of maturity a seed per mile. It establishes ideas when washing a clean-published city of maintained feasible works.

10. Despite antagonism, the light of your implied works poisons psycho-dynamics of interpersonal participation packaged propagation precludes anything sensational self-assured checked deals avow conducive.

11. A sharp line of intelligence butters the bread; razor edges of a rudimentary genius know how to trim your good baked treatment refreshments of for precipitated reciprocation fathoms retaught ingredients of particular specialized transparency.

12. When confusion is impeccable and its affecting an insensible enemy recognized as an irrecuperable imbecile fool stalking you, contemplate a thorough arrangement proposal to un-suppress cluttered inundation of activities; afterwards,

your conscience duplex memory stores real-estate items to program a transfigurative ocean of information; such overdramatized hardships administer tools as the direction objective point, reasoned to drown your burden and sail dissipated worry.

13. Leaving the flat intension of numerous case subjects can complain injury, you need to scream physical strength of record overtopped above the distance and a huge pole vault jump to leap across the sharp point of an ineligible error.

14. If a hiker or traveler climbes to the top of a mountain and places a small lit candle on the top, where there is unprecedence no known light the mystery of the bottom, would he be below standing on the ground with other lights of his people? Where would the star, the star of his glory, be on the high pillar of a tree? Or a head resting on the hill of his bed? But particularly a chalice bieth immortalized on a mantle as a student in class on the small chair of the overshadowing chamber steps steep mountains; its glaring brightness mounts encompassing hope of the wilderness that warms his helpless valley under the hands of the clouds.

15. Dreams open flourished flowers that pollinate tomorrow's alienated rich sweetness, surprising devoted anticipation; yet assessed shall then it unravel an open untied gate; stay observant beforehand watchful----several arrayed doors intercess counseling mouths, assigning reserved passages obscured drinking accounts habituated a trialed trail.

16. If I were to say to you... that if you overfill too much sugar into that adequate sufficient cookie batter recipe or

donut, but not the clarified readable amount, wouldn't that treat be horrible and assuredly; not, spoil the behavior of the unpaid mistrusted taste to that goodie of lesson pacified mistakes? Likewise, if a child is forced sour grapes, that of the vine to a broken tree and that bread has not baked normal to the nation, what most value of that child is he or she foremost receiving, to that of the dessert? For is that bread of the disobedient servant and its mind not that ye of thine table above the sour nation whom mouths open money pouches of war? Then the bread flattens, you lost the point of well-baked delight. Because that delight omitted the father of the ingredients and the goal wasn't gained, its righteousness of enemies have surrounded un-hygienics cleaved of clinging souls, the raining of a tree, and the lighthouse.

17. Wisdom is a great gift of theirs, shall be the number of rain that opens the chamber pillars of the firmament heavens, his stars that light his work have read parables authored in the garden of the pages.

18. If ye is a nonconformist, then assuredly an ethical infected conformist forced thorough disorder of responsibility to the propriety of passive undertaking is inimically guilty of criminal sin because they are pushing customs that's been affirmed not regular made policy of mankind shared that they should not defile below nature; those nonconformists will supplicate to protect old righteous decisions.

19. A key held by a person unLOVEd and unlooked-upon open the ambiguous door, the hated unresolved bridge to several caves smiling severely pacified and treated loyally shall tumble in a wet puddle of rhetorical tribulation.

20. Try, to do not approached careless facade mistakes... 1 mistake there is a 2nd prevention eschewed... could cost and undercut a population unsung as a rooster in the morning, or a dove at midda,y would be assuredly not musicians harmonizing spreadsheets of a blanket on top of oceans during the night.

21. A joyful euphoria is the campfire, the warm light of enflaming glad you inhale the heated argument of triumph you are outwitting; the invincible sting of the mysterious cold that bites your doorway will divide the impertinent barrier conducive between the courteous paragraph you unremembered to reference and the acrimonious---easy structure.

22. Excitement is believing surprised you cannot replace, and an open gift of disbelief you do not have time check and to go back from undone cancelled regret.

23. Women who conceive a smile, bear a kiss given to men desire frowning reconcilable separation; and, a marriage is like a boatsman's vessel; if the cast splits as the rock it is the end of the line sinks the ship and the boat drowns, his or her viable chance the marriage survies is when an overturn annoyance fills bulkheads of water.

24. The sinful refuge a heist of the running oxen, little feet so swift for thunder scampering valiant plagues of reinvigorating uncatch thriving passion, invoked in a phase of outbursting different melody chimes psalms that cure kisses of life, and marriages of hugs. This is the master, it is a trees of spirits, and a stone that lifts up many authorities

of past priests and kings winning authority to necessitate command remodeled chambers preparing an objective to set tables of provisions.

25. A pitiful shrink to the case of their proclaimed introgression position limits the vicarious imagination hallucinated, typecasting normal enjoined among encompassing circumstantial situations; they disaffirm confused incongruence to that the misjudged impart allegory emotion of chariots; and to the victor is privileged to pulling submission of their vines, where no households eat root of the spirit.

26. Clothes worn on people need washing, a reason to insult an implied idea is to bless them a fresh start of the sun refilling cleaned knowledge, so do you also need to wash your ways; simple, so you can be as clean clothes and fine garment shamefully much not so be of rags; but, riches of an essential application to continue humanity wasting gone the sin of immaculate wading pools.

27. When you commit plotted murder wrongfully of infantile activity, staged as that the killing off murder of the child's cup of the plant, their fruit of the season, so they can be as a sword to a fortress of the hallow, your hands that of the merciless ungodly enemy do win only sold materials of so self-pity, mockery, wrath, perversion, irritant blasphemy, and treason for a grave whips the backs of the blameless pouring night into thy hands of no m(o/u)rnings, disjoining my disgraceful----truth from troubled evil; your soapy hands to disinfect bacteria and germs, you hath not submission underplayed for distraction of the oracle. Ye assuredly are

enforcing your gaped farther purposes of broken ethic, so do scattered emulation to that I ratify determine developed affect of demand fortification. But, a payment of ingested hygiene, will be pierced treatment engendered; a work so appetizing to sterilizing your advent approach performed from the esoteric platform vividly witnessed.

28. A log is neither a long wooden pole from a tree or a reference guide sheet that inputs compacts bits of vital information, but a comprehensive system of a basic common person, that is the church of nature and a fisherman watcher of the cascading hills. He categorized specifically to whom who records his embarked plans pursued---cleaved uncontrolled modes private of reviled naïve peers private his cave communes property as each a private learner himself taken hark upon poured refreshments each cure of book a library manages.

29. A prayer vibrates magic, illustrates a wish, dreams of an endeavor, outbraves interceding precision accurate of escaping the escapade, leaping the shores, storming the walls, climbing the fences, secures your quest, desires to ride the wind, valiant to swim the oceans, walks the long sleepy journey, embarks smell to establish placement engraved of precedent substantiated record, procures an elective legacy of prosperity, surrenders a way of condoning service to animate palpable actuation to author manufactured miracles.

30. A woodshed houses the equipment of the indefinite servant, the inexorable coinciding slave driver. A heart shields all the tools of a man's survival to the conformity building his library of his prophetic prodigy.

31. If a lamb was misplaced for 10 units of minutes in a 60th sundial length of measure time to the hour, would that sheep ye not be worth more value of 100 years aged patience not changed frozen suspended than 1 day per 1,000 years of valuable sins of the kings and judges in the palace courts? His master would blow the horn to summon him, while winged soldiers offend trees that feed its young of the Earth a dessert than their portion of honey bequeathed to that of spread propaganda, thine would fib to call a quick-snitch rattled through an honored sown lie.

32. A glad compliment treats an upset condition; a neutral healthy argument soothes a graceful character overjoyed of prudent-married content.

33. What 1,000 meter complication you climb to grasp, is 1 foot repetition of progressive impracticable challenges misunderstood 365 days a year; make 12 hours every 24 of the same candle upon the universal desk of the creator distracted of serious offset peace interluded conjoined dedicated conference self-served just for the incorporators simplicity.

34. If and when a student can surround his defenses, with an armor of masked intelligence, paranoia LOVE of transfixed righteous pain blessed upon his shoulders kiss independence to drag the mountains of all world rained on his uncrowned cranium undressed; frantic galvanized armies of the pray dwell astray in the mysterious camps of the forested wilderness, will be, the competition inimical positionecd compromise to subvert the contemptible

game(s), the mischievous indesign facilitation arranges of a mindful crusade contests.

35. Three meals per day doesn't collect a checked faculty of lubricated conflict, that in the auto-body imperfection subject does which detail the adverse problems upmost slept unstayed; 3-hours worked per-every partial coordinated balanced system of performed justice, feeds the married meal of Philosophy, reading desolate calms waves surrounding starving tides flash light of stars wrapped in a satchel unclosed of crooked darkness; maturity shown every year to earn your daily net-kept misplaced record borrowed condition astray is society's antidote concoction of X=Acceptance persecuted of insured subordination. A food menu provides dishes of treats. A book signified unreached notification of the inconspicuous case, states that it is, does, and self-serves an offered glad gourmet compliment delight, sweetens an enriched study candid of a feast eaten a forethought configuration connected harmony a congruent objective calibrates supernormal reconciliation of the flattened earthly bread.

36. One of a master writer of his tongue, flexibly will ask, did you work? If I give you instructions would you not follow through? If I gave you a button would you not dress? If I gave you a stone would not eat moral lesson to be improved? Only then, you'll receive more bread; leave him crumbs, you get NOT another plate, from having fed the stonewall builder crimes for his talents. Do good services and fruit laid there ready, it does send forth to be done, not where it rots still lifeless, you find it many places spreading from the vine, so shall will be of you.

37. One outdone little of many, but to them every other offering of few, enervates belittled disguise of grace and mask shaded principles decide to bury; heartless customs prosecute whole taste to sample viewpoint prospectives so done greedily on the underrated actions, verified of fakes; but regular handfuls administered further carry coals and oil of combustable busy joy.

38. Suppose you had a business, and that occupation is the expert that self-advises the assessments of equivocal troubles drowning imprints of abstraction, what consideration of design would you portray? Wisdom is a tender shoot, and knowledge of understanding is the grasslands, where the heart of the spirit is the same alike teacher assembles the mind of the cities, which are the chief governors of catering merchants, and disciples are trained soldiers by mentors.

39. Devalue doubt, yield essential focus, break the blustery ground cold hostility of the wolves swelling gloated mouth, strike piercible a swiped cringed torture below the legs of spiked insecurity, sheer the blood of the bitter milk that of the cowardly reproached despisers dread spilling drops of dripped spoiled wine storms, cheating a breath of horseback riding mislead confusion; outwit armies offensively recruiting arrangers, testing the indefinite appointed---construct apparatus time assigned corroborated faith doable of avoided misgivings from charlatan confusion surviving off of surrogate collateral vandalism. You or them not of they, assuredly self-intellectual inject sense overpowering the misconstrued---unconscious obversions outwit your unholy opponents whom are the dummy clay stucked graduated as a vigil official's swing bow.

40. An alleged and apparent simple activity emphasizes crusading longevity; it functions a counter-intuition criteria injunction implied, scaring an unpointed wrecked performance experience unfinished of disarrayed tedious qualities; but, precipitous characteristics digress an efficacious resolution capturing serene management embounded and docking the vehicle that dictates promiscuity engineered from sailed promotions overcasted.

41. What a man failed to do, is but a boy would flexably could think as a man that a mature adult wouldn't do is because underneath the sun of the head; mankind has not child of seed to that demonstrates childish-thieves unheard walked another path to be as the dove; however, when you did not give him a house as he so asked in his naked dried livestock his hands the work, you refused to appreciate not to rate his denounced equitable impressions to that of an eagle, but, appropriate receiving the highest achievement esclated skywatchers among owls spot.

42. Drag a tool to fix a despair, drop a challenge to paint a blotted-blamed challenge, irrefragable prevents an ugly risk, close a relationship, open optional banks accounts of compatible companionship, date a plan or pland a date to open turned success into sensibly signals dicate dedicated resources, convert an estimated roadblock intermitted unclear, then check unclustered errors before deviating specifics for proceeding next. When your sight knows its comfortable your feet will breath a response optimistic gratitude composed of walking inside the cordial-interior fortune box of surprises awaken; allowed reward is resting

quant, voiced thankfully around the workable waiting corner physically referencing an acclaimed position opens for you.

43. Disposable and consumable garbage waste is not only released removed junk material jetsam uncleaned of immaculate usage, you are cleansing the poor unwanted disease consistently stalking your agenda, by letting go of compounding confinement distracting disorderly tension, impacting previously anxiety downloaded in your memory computer system; refresh the assigning moments for organizing occupation to acute an assorted order of inundation compression.

44. If a natural preserver was humanitarian, as a gentle soul, the convent of a self-church living as a sluggish turtle and that the apostle took away is extended, but by a stagnant account of service to insult fearless, its wisdom of his wife participated effort for membership purchased strength outlooking his protection, soaks the blood of wine his stars roar thunders of music, the sweat of his sweet LOVE and candles, all that he could feel through the laws of the door that unseal, would that offspring root of celestial son not be rightfully returned thine all tides of the waves? His pockets did not pull out, his shirts are not wrinkled, his pants did not pluck its leaves of age, his wardrobe maintained the longevity unity of their bright colors, his suit mantled upon the forehead of all authority. He did not change, he renewed his shared sincerity to defiance of transgression and his patience outweighed diligent harvest reborn fresh silently quiet of private acquiescent is a holy consultation; he

renounces acquiescence payment of sacrificial greed covering the world out of poverty, reviving sought not selfish theft of mortal immoral carnivore criminals, and he is thine a pillar of nations disappointment to the unadjudicate troubled is a fortress read the towers of his statues; He is the name of glory, a crown no scratch or streak can cry its rock. For that apostle Christilite, professes earnest bravery enormous than jagged thorns and louder of whistling battle sirens all his unfound tribes in the unspotted place mark his territory, a luster of pearled city defeated of gated crooked kingdoms, so will stubborn judgmental disaffiliation of belief homaged to gain understanding.

45. Courage is a temperature garage; LOVE is warm, fear is repelled cold. The calibrated setting of the sun watches all the differences. The breeze of the wind are the beating of clashing waves cracked upon the coves and coasts of the rocks, like horses battering and thumbing sounds of prayer, judging to offend your ascertained problems and rooted seeded depth of defenses smoking fire below the drunken marital eloped asset to un-forethought wroth material land.

46. Him that subdued of them will assess the embarked disengagement of the arrow; he that of him vomits a flinging arrow like a pestering bug shot away indistingushed as lightning chasing victory; he to of whom slaps the hand of the wrathful rival the brash of wicked, ingests no water of book breathed been sown sunken thine mouth, misunderstands a steel tower to wake a vacuous merchant sacred business.

47. Log verification positions walkable hobbies; several occasions of complicated done field assessments overstress work. They acquire risk cruelty to polish character. Do so more as much thous-thirsted earned shared trust, and for as such participative patience is implicative---imperative, this example of coherence is an anniversary reminder to us we ambush LOVE to reincorporate periodic scenarios of tough guidance, and in substitute pursuit plight to obviate flexible decadent entrapment. Expandable undergone moderators believe, saved lean waste and leaped paramount actions gape ranges of dietetic-authentic content of crucial brilliance. If inveighed dissuasion was neither a conscious indefatigable solution, corresponding its practical self-evident pragmatism, such rendered workable statements would configure un-purchased contaminants disarticulate of simple interpretations. Assignees would submission no role to administer assured choices crossed subdued to confront decidable blossoming affirmation. Remember, self-operable physical accounts of public charity propose seldom persistent---project ignorance. Activity behind closed doors to the blindfold of the mind contemplates complication, liable against simplicity and unfound changed fickle dwelling loyal of thine depth emotion demonstrated. Shameful critics would indispose developmental traction indicated in the details written, that thorough displayers all desire a preference to return quality among sovereignties are stupendous pioneer glossaries.

48. If a waterline or pipe is cracked, because it is spoiled free of discipline, yet it distasted to find quenched-thrive for obedience to brake its vow to carry truth, dropping not

a single tear spilled from a water pitcher, or a drop of vapor doused crying embarrassment to admitted wrongful sin melting of the rotting harvest auctioned seasonal transition to mitigate sin---ended, would you ye not shut off the water first, then patch or warp the ward wrapped of the pipe before messaging the plumber? How more really important additional is a handy repairman that closely related to the maintenance helper than that of the patient receiving edification of the superintendent's applications? The pipe is manufactured pure, refurbished clean, and requires instillation of lesson to join the crowd of other pipes that fit dynamicphysics of its composite chemistry, but never replaces change to convert designation to cover connectivity belonging property. The tighter the fit, the model is suitable of institutional mechanics; and taken empathic technical usage of fatter the fitter irreversible care is received, because the aqueduct pipe channel tube outside of artificial technical nature, has not haste; however, has announced silent-shown scars of pain spoken.

49. The light of their high contrast crown for glory is a smile the highest mountain of kind fragrant vintage, topped the redeemed LOVE recovered... and shall grant them many wives, husbands, and children. Their cup will be payed the enjoyed bed dowery of inheritance, and the hand taught the roof above chastens a chaffed tongue to action of stitched war and house of instructions wage.

50. When you go inside a door, you forget yesterday and wash the dishes of the upsetting gunk that disinfected days passed, but you also remember the unclean mistakes you

discharged trouble named annoyance. You leave where you are, but not out the same door, which indicates that you are no longer the whole person worse then yesterday and that was the 1st door an inch slower towards leveling complexity you did not want to continue, but the 2nd door you climbed that wall through a new door of the temple-mountains to change the disarray unread seeds in the minds of both door of temptable eyes. A door opens when the light of your candle sparks a solution, a light switch shuts off when that trapped door is closed confined of blank concepts-unimagined; however, you must not petrify that assignment in according to ascribed assessment assorted, especially to keep the switch open as the key that opens the door gives treatment a song that cures discord.

51. Books and of what minds make captain of councils, but warrior oracles of forest... they are but a few of travelers and few hand picked, a bit of silver for your horse, a piece of gold for your ail thus drunk road block of quest complete of covering and fine lining to composite the vicarious image of a king.

52. Music, its harmony melody spirit is a generator, dynamics empowers uplifting ingenuity of the author, a creator that tells a story self-directs quality shared of it's character drama. Music speaks chronicles, fables, accounts of events, methods and illusions of escapade planning adventures.

53. 1 teaspoon of pity can cost you a day, 1 cup of shame will despair you discontinuous per year; unless you read the refined lucid facts of those instructions called surroundings, these neighbors argue critical obedience

and recess irreconcilable disposal; dismounting difficulty from wrongful advise of those who travelers trespass know not themselves; reaffirm assurance upon among associated happiness is received the rightful dosage of and reserving justified LOVE shown authentic, thereof demonstrating provided care of dramatic taste participated.

54. If a butterfly landed on a leaf, or a bee on a flower is that one small animal not doing its job contrary rather buzzing or swiftly gliding around society's mischief, not bothering antagonism guild unprotected from helpless preys and alienated risks upon as furthermost slayers, offering gifts to teach its home compliance the world disciple of thanksgiving? Consequence dictates insolence, but loyalty foreshadows overreach earn from gain. Then that insect is pest no more, but a wind of expect to win best founded favor to the successor.

55. A mentor's wrath will never be unbroken, his robe will never torn, a father's ruling policy firm feet ingrain rules of rock will not be shaken wobbly, and a foreteller's liberty that does justice of decree is silent ye not, and thine lord is majesty whose power granted submission is never unbeatable comparable, struck up sharp clashing waves spreading over ocean riptides.

56. Courage is a temperature gauge, LOVE is warm, fear repels cold. The calibration settings of the sun watches all the major---priority difference the dissipation frantic generosity a nonprofit stomach relives quelled envy. Women who conceive a smile grant bigger grins of interest, a 2nd helping of hobbies, and refill glasses of periodic appointments,

surprising a kiss of the fingers and recorded baking undressed intimacy bite of spiced monogamy and hugging the payment of enjoyment sprayed in a communicate fragrance of melted enlightenment blossoming of flourished seduction.

57. If a piece of bread was missing, particularly that loaf then it has gone away; but hospitality is granted faculty of that item sought, the bread would appear however left---resided; a seeded particle, not that to be a grain lost or unseen. It is the memory, the lesson of first assignment you did not cover has to be stored and holding award of the dinner supplicated amiability for guests of the house to arrive and the garden of an annual season hibernating starvation nullified salvation visited.

58. Usually it is urgent as recommended treatment to self-estimate one's eased transition per time carefully by modestly ceasing where you are, and remembering the activities you delayed inaction desire you did not do; the abilities you have clearly contemplated generate a forethought to the furthermost random decision you shouldn't instigate, awakening when least unless insight of dreams convoke crossing that choice dispatched of aiding service helped.

59. Leave behind a house or a horse, you have bread and a family propositioned. Give a shilling, a coin, and fortune you will be benefited credit of loyalty, hospitality, pertinence, courtesy, honor, obedience and grace riches of tongue and and the lips that sail unity collapsing mountains of nation into removed valleys of rubbles of the caves, baptizing kisses in caverns.

60. Legends speaks serene undertones of awaiting mystery, communing speeches from volumes of disciplinary dedication of screaming immeasurable weight, unified for loyalty for a firm asset role. Myths of horns parading pervading cries of surprises; chronicles evoke incursions of ambiguous marveled characters; therefore, as you avid turning the light switch on or pass the green light indicator, coincidentally the doodling pen is authoring its imaginations of in your hand, as feet to walk vicarious prints approached swiftly running an impeccable escapade of capabilities, mapping out patterns for optimistic hope; that you so not also grieve reap wither dry waste of the unfinished but ripen an open tulip of glory, a lamp of sunshine that does thoroughly increases, but do also prophecy of numbers of lengthened rope stretched hammer, waking leaped disgusted mercurial and ambivalent judgment; overhead written water paragraph lines flood material miracles, blotted blighted edifice assurance that of in a swelling bunk of a book, history of his unmade bed, and unrest will untwisted the crooked-core rescued precluded wretched unworthy.

61. If a leaf is loose and floats below underneath the umbrella frown of a tree and as a feather to alike a bird on a separated-unfamiliar neighbor needy of knowing demanded of valued comfort, he of to whom particular has been laid not unstopped worked most, resets and ascends mindful understanding by reached hands, thous a merchant oiling dressed lore disassociates exile for their consulted team of groups severely reproached serious revile for him as his shroud cloth forethought received taken only investment of nuisances embraced. Then would that abstruse servant

be reprieved insult not, be none eventual devoted spotlight significant appropriation devotion too? Then, who is to call last and first of that servant outnumbered rank insecurity disarranged order his turn relaxed of the slave? He to whom-who is patient has overmaster humbled humility, anoints the phenomenal joyful blessed shoulders, granted permissibility chance content employed of fierce excursion of migrated dignity aspired herald.

62. LOVE prays payed effort applied when unanticipated of implied experience transmits apparent, and that drinks a beverage of inception of self-willful evidence conventional of winning a transitioning student to as the alleged transformable master. Fill the dry calm-cool clay potter jars, thirst quench a new song sung played the mud blasting blood in the skies, thundering smoke releasing arrowing fingers each keynote a harmony justifies consuming their fear slept offense averted backslide wrong of accusing innocence. Raining sharp sword replaces the decaying dead of the disappearance unratified incompetent ignorance, sowing shut laughable aversive hypocrisy unavoidable gone begotten vaporized unchecked. The authority part and place put incorporation to reclaim ensuing sprang sheep dragged out wanted as cared and gripped obtained to of the hand in the blood surges the rush of the prospector's saddled horserace executing warranted deployment of the hillside battlefield. That carnal case to of that in which at play is among the supernatural messenger, a dish of sacrosanct reverence inducement names the flattering terror of holy caution going frontward rode on the ensuing indefatigable wind crucified of indefinite boundary the compass directs

valiant fortifiable duty, which fate regulates a consulted doctrine.

63. A door of a chamber is as mouth of a visage quencher, filling concession above inside your hands to robe juice, a bandage covers your wound closing the eyes of gruesome unpleasantry; and a mouthful of fortune cannot easily do simply justice as instructed, if oversize property is eliminated not; a portion of overabundance is enough borrowed to submission allocation ubiquity among the nations, your crowds, and invited guests, then does so knowledge of coordinating stability cleans thine overloaded unsealed junk overwritten, adjusted reserve for the immaculate moral, estranged census cohere an intentional uprise discordance which clouds among eyebrows of the Earth; where which therefore so in my conjunction of council I appoint, there's extinct places of misery unnoticed, not inspected for dealing the sorrowful grumbling those of the hurt scowling impatient bellies that do roar recuperation, plundering the unmatched towering villages gone a cobble stone overturned and plunged aside inexcusable resolute requirement.

64. Abide through the authority wings of the tavern house and your trembling distress uncertainty will unquestionable disappear, that like of a rock exfoliating sheer-scalpel of the shredding disloyalty misplaced peeper. The sediment of spry ruins carved by the flashing arrow of the almighty's pen, chiseled in the breezes, or the moaning of the whistling grass---fields that dwell flourish root epitome grounded palm of the adult; the spice of the foolish characteristics' denouncement disassociated the pitiful shameful, disjoins

them in of the announcer from upright advisors. Gloom migrates apologetic potent fragrancse sprayed-kiss pollination, for ferocious empathy fissured is as the loud crackling holler flicking the slammed flapping holes over the firmament. Booming lightning dismissed doom reflects attention smoked of the wick standing from an overcomer watchmen.

65. Amazement although of the miracle salesman commands feed to the sending of the doves, the chapel of the perch, clasps binding---jurisdiction fastened scrupulous tasks, to befriend humble homage of valiance, an underestimated gratifier is conducive from of for ascertained grace that this applied clemency be unloosened probated LOVE offered to them. They, the eagles do thine yield appendage enjoined seat much yonder socialize preferences; upon thine features miraculous skill coats a clawed slept vision frozen of thou hardened inadvertence; drive, undeserved busy owing purposed promise to diminish nonbelievers, entities assessing accessibility to observe balance weighed of the truthful.

66. A thief buys his own lies stolen through reckless unchanged misdirected material corresponded astray, loft untaught from unfixed conversion from the avoided subcultural; whom, sacrifices the annoying irritant a dispensable volcano caldera and replenish to from of the slippage offset burden-bothered finked ruffians outsourced their cancellation from incompatible differences; an intelligent dealer steals sufficiency of a borrowed ear depositing cogent vegetation crop content sight to his side,

so do as does teaches them to reproach the ungodly statues disconnected of tripping the branch of carved memorial of the leafy castle.

67. Because you dispelled uninvited wroth, evoked do so you wish engendered disbursement upon thine condition burdened-shaken-shockable strife and stiffen discord a defiant suspension of contemplation physically wretched appalled, a despaired account of migrants carried shared shaved misery; understood nevertheless, yet interceded specialized surrogate gLOVEs worn avid interpreted designated preaching, be then would at least disposable potential bitterness depart; a kept-keen thine trouble destiny once masochist misshaped chance and obdurate of opportunity is cleansed challengeable-free dawning refill of the winepress, and is promised unto earned so protected ye are offended not none more again active not returned. You have read, but you have also listened to what I have spoken having pampered detail, my flow of encouragement that of intended meaning for you to as flexibly recover retrieved chore expectation once begun taken thee upon thine incorporation; receive my transference treatment I determine to repent saving treats of my contrived chosen recipient hosts; you so as seriously be additional good of subdued relation under my order, praiseworthy regarded unbothered by woes, anchoring a controlling disease from the inept product of feasted recommendation so you are experienced to revoke wolves bitting your natural program, preventing critical cynicism of chomping teeth seducing confusable adverse trespasses.

68. I grant just cause of the hearers for among all of you decided approached continuous----inconsistent rivers of ambiguous eternity. Condone my preferential proposals procured to dissuade a key I saved for you, so a door also magnifies its open majestic treasure, you twisting the doorknob of the world; the message of thou myself and inspective servants heed many proficient languages; unless otherwise suffused distinct, that you'll be emancipated of us. I will prosper you recourse of catering hope, justified a balanced case of my loving devotion done service assigned; so, you're concisely experienced and assertive of these precedent-possibilities for opening unrolled scrolls.

69. Investment of life, ye do work achieved patience unpriced nations cannot configure dispossession, but you also know conflict of reason provided incision and thus I do also commissioned my ambitious predesign made confession, surrogate enhancement manner of this truth, that these things applied mouth of buried nourished distempered of evaporated spiked-thorns corded recession removed. Interexchange substitution is inevitable, lies down perhaps to wipe the tears held adorability of the demised valleys; otherwise, goal-gaining purposes to the thinkable attainability to reach better; a contained passage of irrigated fields not with wine but elation fountains of rivers drowning moisture from fathers do a much so a lot. Told you, in ways done mentoring through a guider and regular issue encumbered blockage so strong authority is ascribed, you be glorified benefaction given-collect shall have because honored parent and the child composited a sip of thirst clarity; that both each in such is as equatedequitability

shown accountable account reliable emulation, and that of rank high apples plucked by the hungry gardner below, no longer rotting is he, but the oncoming fresh product materialism---platform an oncoming enriched product assessed and central observation is a vivid pragmatism commuting commenced beautified harmony of winning trees.

70. "Sin conflict, yet done as what upon perpetrated physical fallacy upon thine touch affect, what was is not, and never shall be again and wasted dissipation demise oder of a bloodthirsty war of irrepressible-work battle orchestrated much overdone; be hark thou shun scorn deliverance surrender to sour obscenity, beed and string clean and be contained present not; reborn of a messenger, so sent a message is the witness arraign assemblage core of the announcing incorporator."

71. Bandage a, ice cube chilled drowned of a vintaged beverage you deepen ties rose buried below forgone curbed animosity, which everyday you mediated the smokestack of thine lungs rectified taming-leveling score of a misanthrope encroacher. Stitched justice giveth colluded amuck hence sung a written noted melody treatment beheld handful grooming of egregious patch retired suckedbreath impotent ground disappoints vanquish relief registered; cover gnashed jaws plucked shaven---smooth amidst thine innocent lad youngling for voided capture placated narrow, justified approval stipulated a surrender, and hugged gain retribution miserable argument of mindless scapegoats amputated hostility towards appeased occupation busy

fruited satisfaction, prevalent guilty volunteered of charity welfare; abide hostile quelled bribed institution, features a sunbath faculty principle undone. Broiled actions assign smirks authored roasted narration, therefrom content tutored, necessary of generous sermons migrated. Perform 3 amicable inscribed assessments urged usages of useful utilities, rarely but importantly irregularly common to clean, change, convert, delete, rewrite, read carefully and check lucid understandable work. Based on a series of 3 basic core dynamics, categorize a vehicle desire of exercising these tools. Apply the 3MS (Media System) responsible-regulation, model, method, and medium from the adult platform of ingenuity insight. Your 1st utility element you model is a cooped viewpoint begun by a diagnostic basic assessment agenda, assigned by escaping a complex approach. 2nd simplified utility element you import is method... execute your plan, decide if the precedent circumstance is a reliable scenario instance of in the judge scenario, then trust the pointed path you you. 3rd comport utility strong to ascertain is a medium, the idea structure you step, and system you leap is justified arrayed accordance dictated of timely order coinciding a facilitated choice.

72. Your work will not rent open house for that earnest security of warm, unless released is an efficacious pheromone impression added to the increased dosage ingredient melded the charge, challenging intermission regulated temperature envied opponent's distempered complicity eschewed contained evaded contrite.

73. You've overcommitted dedicated patience, personified charismatic decision clothed deduced as paged read hinged clinging drapes for ringed imagery at the highest conceived towering projects a toe per inch; follow further throughout---thorough invested assurance profits as to understand. Counter-contrary else, enable a fortress wall peak unbreakable test of notation, built suppling materials of redundant dexterity ambiguous distress enjoin mighty a discussion to indispensably transfere a volume collaring obedience. Fuel your glowing lantern discussed upon the ways standing in the way as the purity of an apple; a disciplinary deadeye stare cautions the frantic paranoid scourger a struck match.

74. Some handful of audiences crowd incapacities of incoherent incense, and cannot see the rising sun from the mountains. Others assumed other another among a few least overhead, cannot distinguish therefrom up the light over the forest trees.

75. Feed a fool fish they will still swim away, give a mindless child spoiled fruit, they'll still be rotten assuredly and intellect has the fool knowing how to fish.

76. Your pen is your magic wand. It sincerely gestures real preferences; the world you build in your hands writes buildings to house towering worthy protection enforced. Immune-risk dangerous consequence among action warned performed impeccable, obviate atruse contentious and inimical adversaries of people from insinuating---insubordinate atrocities shone illumination, hydrated enchantment animated held for the other sequel quote per-purchased

better artists. Confine non-conformed passion, humble, and do thine gracious acts of mercy prepaid order to thrust pierced disorder thrust condemnation of the helpless; the prosperous rivers of seas and the crystal eyeglasses of lakes naked-candid thoust affront apathetic abandonment of their receding negation; thou of thee thine not hath has drank hugged return of the ponds' oasis sooth relaxed taken upon the grips of the steam wrapping babe, encompassed the blanket horn melody harken, for heath safety closure of a child, the discord lamentation desolation under heartache grieved thine housekeeper unforgiven imperative, the upriser constitutes his ascent of the monastery to the hilltops.

77. As the sight of your world, both father and son featured seated aide the statue of the face, the observers gawk intrusive testimony these passages of passive reliable truths worked does calm fine interminable drought cleared characterization typically found checked that of a book, a letter of a few healing instructions; name of what he is and does as a cometh outwitted calvary imbues resuscitation anointed holy of inviolate crued breeded knighthood to announce the acclaimed submissive glory harvest season vineyard plucked crushable predilection appreciation and gauntlet sampled sipped dry soaked dismemberment fruit amidst rose shed glorified famine; so, sung only as lifted high hath cordial gratitude, thus thine disestablished unnerve misshaped hopes of strung apostles, rejoiced revived supper delivered; and, caught-carried dripped crammed requires thee risen defense-climbed the mountain of the prophet; but he whom thine affirms statues according such a prevent-precarious fall reclaimed invests enlightenment, the laws of your cherished advantageous habitant format.

78. We pray for the least woes, and wish at last the most upmost condemned torn mouths ripped rooftops of the churches burden. We as of believers dress our sorrows, to frustration so as it doesn't insult eviscerate argumenst disgrace uncertainty of leveling a way viable of private priority.

79. Pungent oder of blustering unforgiven blame threatens inaction sanction of progress engineered tongue hammered of a hobby readapted proliferation undone, unless thine threatened surrounding guilt confiscates voice talent, but hath garth no consideration joined truce homage yonder spluttered sprung bathed intolerance pregnant of helping good thine LOVE ointment shave---silken polished done straightforward the duality of granted discharge given.

80. The taste of backsliding held patience is a preferential missionary appointment, thou suitable self-accomplished from intolerable balance for hungered completion, avoidably opposite of disavowable contest, the incessant mistakes born thine twins called them, for of they thou are of them are known as insolence and frustration. The fussy restless gradation is below the bottom belt points explicable warmed fire of basic instinct; assuredly it is mislead when naturally sensible a straight forehead where fury does not write of that 2 variant inequities to of a farm from the pen of the valleys efficient records.

81. What is wisdom? Same spirit as understanding; what is courage? Same messenger as strength; What is hope? Same traveler as glory; What is fortune? Indistinguishable maturity from Philosophy? What is power, where what authority is of

as and is also at where your heart is held by a watcher, refute degradable a doctor that has a soulful spirit not, because he's misunderstanding a sick inescapable fate outwitted from of chanced reformed LOVE that's contagious of the fearful spirit.

82. A thief believes bluntly the quarreled acquired attitude and displeased incongruent evasive adjustment in unregulated impact, notified conformed deviations aloof stripped gauge ripped laceration rejected transitory redemption for nothing; but not however nonetheless, affirm if thou traitor of kidnapped flour, is the wheat of salt the souring transformed procured sinner from justice in the family attempting entangled abound constriction divested tongue striking a wick of illuminative shadow, beamed a surrogate spotlight gloated upon onto among foremost a galemocker of troublemakers. A guilt felt patronizer gaped erroneous from the demeanor of a watchful look, the projected thrusting a piercing stabbed arrow, the biting mouth of an ugly sight determining the ambiguous metaphor in the camp of a desert, the steepless pine cones shed thistles left in the tight crevice of aisles.

83. Support aside the kissable care of suffering grieving audience, your neighbors candidly grieving impetuous desperation to be hugged under the arms of the dew that is caught by the rose of the wine, the waiter who also sits head-master above the guesthouse dinning room of the banquet. Reconfigure inviting earned credence to the ownership in your hand considered certainty in their position, staying valued to the built-room of their assistance in the effort

space of your room rented a thought to engine a dictated encouragement and obtuse obviated removed misdoubt to rain annoyance of blessings notified significance commanded sympathy as a hand shaken. Also, access done work migrated, so management can disinfect a hygiene policy case obstinate stubborn easy through every contaminated action commanded.

84. A cup fills your hands robed majesty; a throne that builds benevolence amidst the charged investment imbues efficiency, that of a project immodestly indefinite its assemblage imported aspect poured below bottomless famished plates and services nourish an invitation, features a menu of understandable quotes each envelope opens another day's moment selected arrangement assigned to be covered a test; and the assessable clouds fill wells to heal higher, and unclogged rooftops stronger vapor boasts thine burdens exalted mercilessly sobbing the distraught mists lift forces off of you, scattered of restless indecisive activity plans thrust its unplugged jars. If for aren't thou been rebuked inequitable hydration unmatched overturning village furious antagonist provokers, impossible digestibility has breach stomached upon a holy barricade; they cannot themselves reach contemptible ploy, a bled quicken extraction recessed a clanked outspoken vitriol to slice grinding misery.

85. What line you throw, listen, and follow me and then you focus famished being replenishe more fish will abound to your side, but a fish you will not that of a serpent but some bread and rock with a name to your sword of the spirit and shield of faith.

86. I shall cast my sheep a line, and fish to catch captured saved exceedingly exalted a much that my children be reeled from despai,r and to my lambs that dwell in my book, a life written on my tree forever.

87. I weeped and mourned, but flourished and extolled magnified, because obtained mercy upon allied applied legion commendation willed allegiance fostered to make sour my test, so my challenge sweetened when bitter I was looking for not, and stronger zesty the obstacle greater taste outsmarted the fouling pungency of undetermined irregular scared pollinated virtue scented inaccessible to dare.

88. Those who save souls, a brightened wick is conserved and many more assuredly glorify. Themselves, a student contracts a skill because this is righteousness is operating; this allusion explicit is the architect owner of taught talents. The exaggerated twinkled star corresponds, projected excellence is massaged a container of immeasurable peace exposing the basis surrounding the years in sections of the page capacitate, gladder the candle cools, and greater good greeted are is to those who carry aspiration of from among interpreted that content, distinct expectation conviction a promise of an admired corresponding message is brought surprised use.

89. Seldom periods predict the suitable circumstances to find what you're exploring to obtain, is least best not to look for such complicated mysterious things at all, but naturally let what you're searching to arrive particularly among for of you proven upon you depends criteria decided done earnest reception accurately gained.

90. Patience invites a tenacious universal anniversary of celebrated remembrance, obediently insubordinate and sufficient to poison expendable indefensibility robbed from below underneath of your shortcomings; discharge prudent wrath excluded, preventing meedled and muddled adverse levels advancement kissed invincible.

91. Be smart as the dolphin, be fast as the wolf, be elusive and mysterious as the tiger, be brave and courageous as the lion, be strong as the ox, turn and develop as the hawk you're light of impounded justice, therefore compromised of impartial balance but weighted authority of the skies, so that the fence of your wilderness is built steep above the safety columns of a mountain, drowning profusion disjoined of thine inequitable outclass dissidents, and where they do not drink techniques of primitive instinct climb the bowl to outrange dwelling of the hilltop and to then further envy fury expedited of to the adored proprietor label discerned authorizer.

92. The better-bigger-greater credible capacity weight emotion recorded effort maintained accountable of your gifted skills, the hungrier exaggerated LOVE often will classify brought---sought truth banked riches stroked luminescence nurses returned intuition facilitating contribution for constitutions scalple institutions.

93. Observe true LOVE as your friend, commune council of to your neighbor for thou greater gracious houses many friends in the house of a holy alter, later, a ladder the risen capture fish of a hand, a fisherman's catcher's rod and inherited then enormous fathomed---featured affirmed a

fortune; for passionate conviction champions additional memorabilia, endorsable limitation, adamants incompatible among compliances much distinguishable prestigious services, also depositories wealth a much factor expansion wedded landlord constituting piety commitment undercut redundanc.

94. A recruiter would received the finest fish your stomach can marry worn fish handled, the finest hoard harvest below the dug hole drank approved satisfaction admired a garment polished graduated instruction. A member obtains deduced strain contracted recovery inflicts received treat decency tasted items rained arms masking his body. Unless, particular oil of anointment essence fragrances self-controls obedient caught escape tendencies, nearly compounds hath obstructive conception harken reserves of a caped-robe figure ascertains dreams possession safe sanctuary quarantined.

95. A poisoned mind is a defiant ambience time---wasted worthless problem obscure of the world; a Philosophical imposed impression unmade assured licensed deliverances qualified eligible standards overrunning an impractical character-base implied unapplied intelligence.

96. A bird cannot fly unless it is immoveably dispatched a parked position, neither can you the apostle if stopped scared of protested conflicts forgiven, unless, judged a condemned begotten sanctified inaction is assented confrontion mediated a truce. If at thous least must reset, ahead go, and rework the issue ingested the intellect to dispel the soaring disguise swept below your eyes and wiped swing above other opposite distinct infliction weighed down its despicable

chaos voyaged inexperienced a paralyzed base gravitized, especially a tearing grievous sin. Irreducible discord coughing misplacement of its wing, where feathers demise suffusing propagative separation a lightning symphony; a deaf mute in the mysterious night aloud breath stars sung sirens, alarms tranquil symphonies.

97. A lamp that has no scripture can not light ambiguous soliloquy of preached light, for if that good light has no base below the belt of the pillars, then assuredly the pillars will not become towers and fortresses will not luster bowls and dishes for lanterns brightening laughter and risen fortune---esteemed doors of a letter opened beauty of saints refracted of dust and sand, so doves can escape to eat more of a revitalized sun pointing a translucent arm of housed rooftops.

98. Taken hath begotten embedded principle conceptuality scatter, that does so do fathom characteristics communicated simple smart incorruptibility dressed for, and cover embraced much dress promote ideas dubitable. Discomfort uncloaked naked mouths, disfavor inept ingenuity of rivers reviled ungodly rivaled ropes that profuse unaffordable regulated mouths, ripping horrendous shred honeymooned infestations itemized many refused undone preclusion according of conformed compliance; unresisted precedented option changes an easy assessment assembling collection in a filtered attitude ascended of balance worn triumph that of an adorn brillance worn.

99. Oblivious demeanor dwindles a criteria cleared of a obscure forests, therefrom determines the wasting

disappearance of clotted fur overcasting clouds smoking outreached inhalation madness drying the dripping wine off the stems, cut disjoined overcast holes of the fields in the firmament horrifying dug retribution reckoning blood retuned praised truth to a fallen wanderer; he for as his once him, did grant a sleepless unrest separated underground the ceiling of a far apart elongation an unclimbed extendable ladder permiates associated effort of rescue.

100. If somewhat perhaps a small vine holding a branch is disjoined a one to many thorns short, to that of basically an essential thistle socket left a gem stamps a sticker to a garden covering the stomach of his people, they will not eat the main---course of warning tasted a bit of an ear imperative the last point; neither, will anyone remain of if thou assigns pervasion hunt to obtain a mightier traveler is still standing, then rebuild the wounded stamp lifting a warm wounded arm nestled mediated mended hence forthright straightened chargeable mandate hand, that among upon carries content clutched drinkable fountains bellicose communicable wraths doomed thy blood sipped containing one's purposeful accommodations.

101. What difference is one discerned be of a shark and a fish? Fish prevent to do notpulling the fisherman's line on the wizard's right wand, if the staff of kingship is the welfare condition of the people a carpenter constucts; however, sharks on the other left hand snap, bite, and crack derisive antipathy if you misuse catching the wrong faith to repel them forevermore, a can or sealed bottled jar been filled of mastered bait.

102. Judge precedented readily way-well avoided evasive-trouble, only privileged… pass sadder of good meal, fortune of delicious taste, and food of thanksgiving so you judge be that of the earnest approver-approached that you devour my earnest trust, and receive again life of thine for receiver of good will towards mankind, unstuck to flow the river of unconfined contention of disconcordant-distention tranquil again.

103. My tomb will outburst to speak, not to exemplify insensible clarificaiton not, or waste lazylounges of beforehand the prudence that I initally comment gestured roth madness, or dispairsinful rage outwrong rebukers rage, but rather whisper quiet patience until upon the miracle the sky eats a purpose maketh responsibly to prophecy fate fortunate content arrayed of the judges robe. Coverage the drinketh light firmaments, hung blesssed---blossomed salvation the doth fool wrangler undebted exonerates impractable seducious dust, for of a loft leaped agone inhalation the anxious trembled misery a tiresime-striken assistant is an asset.

104. A flown baptised admissioned obligation is a messenger parisions of their pentences traveled above the helper's retentive sown-planted blatbbath confession premised.

105. Isecured peculiar propaganda mirrors perceptive as such perseverence amount grasped, practically rejecting discombobulated rude criticizism fortified did, that I matched, outbeat, outsmarted, and mastered the wickest moments unbarriered that I sufficed in a scuffle.

106. I will divide the tears of the oceans, as sailed slid the waves wind stairs that the trees walk on rivers. Consequently, subsequent pessimistical prided effort will be embarassingly complimented, as dried fortune glooms an unshaken gleam for the unstoppable sinisterness nearer to as the righteous unweakened trails of unsold baksets, and then have not their stomachs glorify the grace a promised tree cares for shedded undone spineless and shared-sharppend renouncement is unrejected.

107. Your worthwhile you have with yourself will never sunset dehydration of an oasis because, sin has drained below the speechless cracks, an illusion untamed and replaced in thirst sipped through your doorthat no one can close or open the cave walls with your own laws you write poured in the church above the blessed crowning forehead.

108. An artist out of business that trained the architect to certify the doctor licensed to drive crazy on the jagged road, every essential ubiquitous corner budded and poppied infallible misdirection points is unsure poisoned under obscurity.

109. My tongue will gallop fierce burning coals of fire, opening ministry to open exilation opined howl disguised disgust, that horned on a chair sat a cup rest slept drink below the river abyss, that depts are sound-planted ears voiced wails in the torn houses. It rocks, stormed ships torn garments of secured material overdressed wrapped bravery stern upheld mounted the vessels, are positioned unshaken of beneath the shorelines.

110. Several many birds have unsung, where the trees whistle unsaid remarks fruited grown opinion, the rivers and lakes stilled filling their harmonies, the mountains have blinded as the facade folded concealment obscured uncertain as their ambiguous apathy scolded wrath quickened its unshaken resentment; the clouds have hidden overcast, invisible disappearance all become as it was, is, and will be quiet the judgment transfused saving of lives, hand-deliveres madness pacified cured and redeemed hath LOVEsurrendered.

111. Yield traffic of bills, overdue payments, and expensive of utilities returned of debt charge payments cancelled, stop during traffic limited a specific certain uninsured instance scenarios; however, but dramatically as during car pooling season hourly profit wisely captial dispensed, when indispensibly owing the borrower and principle loaner equally reciprocated back to the originator claim lender.

112. Bravery is priceless, done, and because courage is mislead muscle pressured tenacious difficulty often specific troubed wayward at times; and because it is layawayed, coincidence usually begins through skillful thought consciously fathomed through a voiced reminder to gain an idea, entailing sensient goals primarily, "I will think about it," secondarily "I'm going to assess that sample," last and third aboutly ascertained the philosophical accessed concept concluded "I've heard and seen the facts about this plan, therefore monitering this general idea provided is a great solution reached; I've indicated my decision whether organizing shrinkage of a extra bulk storage cluttered in a small tightened room, a business, leniency-leasure for

time encompassed around my job or work, or 5-10 year short ironic of long-term interceptive purposes to do finish that busy work." So basically, yes I trust I will overreach conclusion discontinued candid once and eventuate the task done with self-confidence obediently bought.

113. The sooner the freakest fools deceitfully confess their misjudge sins, a cup of salvation will anoint their kissed baptised lips rubbed-in bridged dishope to a bedded care and quality of qwelled forgivness inconsistant blamelessly adjouned unreasonable distressed arguments.

114. An oasis infreaquently, but usually predicted its self-minded basis wastes sacrificed natural resources to save a disheveled discipl,e if the oasis is the unrugged is a coherent benevolent kindergarten cherish-incorporator, while a mirage blinds the fools confiscated, nothing exportes a crop packaged until unreserved- depleted and abound-abandonment anonomity parents of an unoccupied barren-shaped trival enitity is outspoken finished analysis.

115. Subject a tire to pain of a wrecked road, the tire will be slept and age passsed a meal carried across superficial substance shared alongside the table is broken apart; because, there was no doctor an urgent standby to treat the road that built the nation, as the child who is badly placed the ungrown chastened his resolution to subject repair.

116. Your inflammed enemy is not your rival, dismemberment of the position to empty scarce poverty is scarce and scarce harassment dissipation disinfected of survival, and the inherited condition is fine; otherwise, the

subject is the light upon receding discombobulation; As the agenda forget paramount fright of impossibility and when desired resources needed as when, it, and then, shall will hence happen.

117. It's not a our place as people to offend our enemies when they the fierce rivals hold you begrudged frightful possessing something; but prudently, knowing all wise they concede no position to defend themselves from our own authority of creator accounting anything noting. A handshaken kiss of peace, LOVE, and warmth is their weakness, they know it as why smiling and happiness, jokes and laughter is their weakspot and enforcing euphoria as illegal, so give it to them... give and your place will be positioned all reunited... and what you are provided more wonders will be accomplished.

118. Your intent is not alone to be in weakness to that of excuses fused, but rather fousted fiercer virtue rendered of standard career evaluation of work record transcripts that dilapidate---distiguishiable reliability and extinguishable defusability, so these methods of tools refurbish expertised friendship valued comprehensive abundances greatly appreciated the application of ample dependability.

119. Sink important gravity to the incorporated-provided and plundged of performed blameful inaction guilt righteous, subtly impartal but yonder delicate prudence subdued unbothered; stern a stormed embraced scene of restrained undepressed action, and checked affirmed to proceed accessible effort impressed implied account with

manifested exonerated worth justifed its signified dizzy innocence.

120. Your prospector trainer is not your wasteful type, the unpardonable spectator opposite assembling arranagment of the contestor; the quintessence obstacle is yours alone assigned bequeathment for you to overstrain the suspected microscopic challenge, lighting lucidity quickens understanding purely soft to ferociously uncontolled stubborn unfriendliness, stays true underneath overstated strong nature and sustains conscionable unquestion to mirror a polished man spruced of loyal character.

121. Funny, faith has 3 doors: 1st of the those doors is you remember the moments you didn't fill the pitcher of water, the middle door is the instance that you maybe shared your glass with someone worse self-senseful from acts of severe pertinence and else because they were sicker, and the final door is the door that will never be closed because your payment has been settled and surcharge covered and recorded for delivering your thankful deed to that person.

122. A small mustard seedling can shake the world, and difficulty would outrage the mountains that confine grasp of the glass pillar; a tinier barley grain snowflake can embrace control for remorse, eased gripped otherwise edgy galvanization and cover the mustard seed winter deaf mute vacated.

123. Gladness favorted as pleasure is a joy, and gratified delight an enjoyment. Paritculary, some one who desires peace and carries his surroundered deliverer under the staff

of his judgment, under his wings; a receiver of knowledge abides to his master. His teacher, is justifed to overtake the fouling fooler, turning the petrified-paniced-manical-mechanism inherited of paraphobia from the difier's face. The apostle abides his place settling to pacify the irreverant genesis, and recording his position to serve the offering of his guilded faith.

124. Apparently, when the case is bothered none or confined limit to compress judged debate on the incense crisped hills of malignant misusers, hypocritical cancer in the private supreme court expansion of social-authoritarianism, is the recipient protege guest of honor arriving in a capitalized vehicle liability claim; a yard per-size measuring damage unannounced is in an unfordable bill, and insured compensation of tax diseases, and a red tongue walked----shuttered of life recoded irreversibly to repeal an irremovable gone impassible form of performed paralysis stops the executive contract disease plagued viral-sprain.

125. Lots of men and women are becoming the couples we never divorced before the renounced breakups, and the acquaintences we renounced wanting to marry; but, consciously separated from our homes and lawns moaned and mowed reproached from our private resources accounts carried in our pockets, faithful charaismatism is easy to clasp that for of the shaman.

126. If you build rocks blocking front upon yonder your batch, if you don't wiseup, put previously recently behind the pressure of mortificationism that builds the rocks that fortify your destiny, legacy will not lossen up burden, and

grief will not dispel to grovel undon and gratified, so you shown improvement shall assuredly accumulate a vision transformed for listening and lifting you to do lessen desires.

127. When someone uses fierce agitation to turn you paranoid, unsettled, nervous, vindictive, insecure, negative, condemn, chastise, and criticize you argumentatively and transform you vaguely unobservant, then the opposite--- oblivious counter-subject is labled the determined breathing drug administering unacceptable tretchery utilizing misunderstandable liability in your eyes, your ears, and in your mind them whom propose an awful purpose intent to mutate you sick; you disallow an evasion to fortify that traverse product you're communing with is unavoidably incompatible from you promoting exposure of spread poisonous risks precluded.

128. Plant him relearned in your life, the cure will rejuvinate the miraculous legs of chariots, and complacent gifts of horses will be apparent of sight, presently reported salvation stampeding your preemenient moviation. Come together, no fear have you not alleged, a not have fright gone anymore clear away modified appearance turned disincorporated invisibility vaporizied, so least assuredly not your thumping heart mortify palpitate is regressed virtueously, but be confined the the martyre's dominance pierced stronghold as sworded victory, thus sealed appendix astride forthgiven overturned wreckless ushered underseiged.

129. He he seals often closer opens delivery.

130. Dripping dropped a small dosage amount of effort encounters an engineered amount of encourage energy. Interjecting married light interlaces life alongside surrogate proteins of reason resurfaces signficant principle.

131. If you LOVE common understanding, you will obtainably find implicity to be likewise and therefore then futhermore common legimate commonality for seducing your protection saved rendered survival in that closed box deposited reciprocation held helped effacious grace, esteemed praiseworthiness.

132. Unique pleasure is enrichly gratified a groom, its joy, and gladness a bride Called sincerity. Particularly, someone who desires peace, and carries his staff of judgment, under his wings; a resurrected redeemer is the receiver of whole paranormal intelligence whom abide universal trustworthy loyalty to his beneath his master's sung engulfed wings. His teacher, is justifed to overtake the fool turning the pertified-panic irritant of paraphophia from blinking the patronized thrushhold of a defier's appearance, confronted unsmug a bewildered evil face. The apostle conclusively abides his affirmed reserved place his mentor delivers, settling to shape clear instictive cogency connects unto the discernable Christilite gentiles, him marked aformentioned to his and he recording his position to serve the offering of this unrenounced immaterial faith.

133. The light in the darkness, a son of all mankind exemplified touched engender reached new felt meaning in the wilderness, fish for my lambs, wine for my stars, so

that the oil brightens my fish and plentiful are wicked a reservation, waiting a chair at the table.

134. Winning the position or job to do a heroic operation or obtain equal placement are 4-levels of persistance expectation allegorical to the characteristics of the interconverting seaons. 1.) You fill out the cold winter application, where you are determined based-cneter around eccentral competion, despite yielding subpractical competition trust. 2.) Elected employees will be chosen so fall into place. 3.) Summerize your evaluation status personalized on a company untility observation and simplify work ethic. 4.) Congratulations you are hired, now don't sit as a jackass, spring into captial action.

135. If presupposed you notice an issue, watch it, catch it, snap it, shutter it, and stop it published by authoring a grant pardoned of your eyew. Now develop those issued negatived reels and taken previous problematic ages done.

136. Knowing what to expect is discerning acception to allow the results, release unanticipated presumed supposability and reveal inadvertent all your intent of coins will build dollars fallen like leaves from a tree, assurdly in your hands, and as well as many confident will exude adaptable consumer benefits.

137. Let the speeder on the road arrive late to work stronger, fortune will dispurse to you early as stangant work is stipulated best graded smart. But your masterpieces are promoted intelligence of blasted brilliance on a lighter platform catered.

138. Demonstration misjudged grate-greeters gather to greet you are and have received already a gracefully giveout, and mutual obnoxious reciprocates grant the gust of the reward gather to incorporate ascribed orators.

139. Antiquity is a rare product centralized as encompassed integrity; the unique basic core is assured quality dignifies a translation applied affirming mutually gratification of the essential qualifiable best standard policy, and dedicated for irremovable authenticity.

140. Display conveyed visibility to the mischaracterized grate-greeters, you are and that you have received already a grateful give, and mutually obnoxious the flow liability of the reward will condense gather to incorporate bigger rejoiced ascribed presenters that honor.

141. You contarily are unworkable to the absurd, therefore thee---virtual impossible and inessential obtained intermission waits, until nevertheless further harmonized phenomanon gratificaition for collected promotion is mothered as a superviser, but ye of where when to start settlement stated from the roof of the buildling your rank level as a specialist undergoes resets initiated inception inscribed as indictaed from the base beginning. So how? Well, where you are the employee of the year showcases overhype spectacle of prestigous surpise so special as your plague there is hanging; so be it your most precious regular freight of cargo understanding is fitted at the roots below the base, and by your first step of the ladder be thereas your roomed cogent foundation. Like a blouse, coat, or formal jacket---the river is buttons up drieness as no thrist is carried

charge of venders dislodging the veins of the Earth, the creek winds predestination all space of the unwritten road. Model a taylor signified viable, but distributed their confidence as immesurablity ascends then for spotlight, sulks-saddened further irritated shipment in hopefulness ears unrecessed is unrested, that none has foregone a dissention uglier any predication hallucination blustered a wind chime, clinging disciplined desperation to a ceiling as wings filter the brusable dazed overwhelmed in a malase dilapidated unplanned obscurity.

142. Moutains can and will not weap, weary moans grieving pettles fallen nurtured begotten lost let left forgotten younger and away far went yonder weithering of like a flower, his will not remains flags of merchant ships tear judgment divorcing the resiliant distinction badged descendency alongsided nearby the captain, cities significantly longways domain territories between subverted boarders will not smudge the clearing fog of a finger lifted off frost, neither cold of spiced dirt on the lenses of spotless lakes or bedding unjustified intersprucable waters; nonetheless, unpresent of rightousess blameness, but seduced by the character hospitablity of purposeful priority to do performed major responsible ajounred attitudesis controlled proper edification. Because, a standing house of the peached voice from the scriptures, fortifies barriers them do immune collapse nails misdirected seed salt on bread; its wrath spun overrun cannot override authority the impressed fortress features the working fortune is doing in the making, and then no enkindled spoken sprout of gold claimed is reopen to that set table like a kingdom of brances; it is on a willow tree untroubled its hearted calm serenity.

143. If a straw was pulled by a member of a recruiting team, and the shortest boy pulled the largest straw, assuredly wouldn't you assign the boy to perform the appointed task to embark the need of the group? Send the lad out into the wilderness, and in "3" days limited unquestionably inconsequent he will return with a medium stick where the straw drawn has gone disposed and a boy unshaken intrepidy has mounted a trophy, as a seen man staffed curtain draped on the brass hinges worn upon thy rare neck like a colorful staineless glass window of a church.

144. Condone the opposite helpful gesture of support to outbrave the unspeakable anxious hassle, contrasting a major conveyed scenario contrarily strainable to confront the hooligan challenger under-controlled rendered truth mutually of a tumultuous---fericious rival is to win the antipathy of the argument; your gift of earning others' self-respect from unique confidence of trust is piloted greatful intiation that has befalled and dwindled thouest intiation, joined-entailed appreaciation. Because, appeased conciliation is reckoned particular authorization a coinciding audacity concurs to glorify significant magnificants pulling harnessed authenticity from the rope of frugality.

145. Solutude prayers of parked conceived sermoned scripture treat you a disclaimed burden that as few and several receive the most discord, that a subpar burn you shall not have possession of that entity, a drink that you have quench dryness your thirst suffering, suffices undertaken much suffusion maintained carries to state... with one wing soaring above, and another brushing below may knowledge

of the brides, grant a kiss and blessings will cover you in stars, an overcast of blight be thy sunshine removes elevated leaves to my shaded garden.

146. Wash your obscure sights from the springs, given least pardon pertinence linen sheets for of warmed your eyes, and disbelieve continually, until actions are done unsaid from undone limited parables. Permit truth through trust to trust change for becoming your siblings. You'll never grieve wine as underwent a drunken burden madness, and bleak premature prominence is a decided criteria scarcely a neighbor rooted buried---blood burdened from blindness dips sampled-sipped discarded overfilled valleys drunk its thirst.

147. Even an apostle will never be accepted in the inner-cities of the villages, but a good root is less bitter that than of the runoff barley and glutton unstirred the purpose of noted messages, translated truth compatible only to my people on the right; as for the mindless, should the shallow wicked never understand because leased lied borrow has unsealed payment bind-biddith-thine is not between a responsible gesture or a glad favor returned, should least assume whom ready that does chose, and a servant does not gone distasted work of his acted light be thine of than other older, then of that I am enteral.

148. If thou has a small stone and you mispreceive its beliefs the impossibilities it does not perform, assuredly it will tighten bigger rocks joined and age, and a loaf of bread will sweeten flavored tastes, because simple rose to the higher

mountain tops of a roof covered its payment of dispensed worth.

149. LOVE can confabulate riddling unrolled notices traveled, singing noted characters, but rudly rejoices the probable additional ways of numbered might; Shined unstoppable dismissel entices flexible endurance of ungone reinvigorating strengths and insulting richness transformed into a composite figure acquired capacities of vendering paragon assessments assigned. A facilitator of insight discharges overwhelmed superintendence curbing foreign undiscovered management. Deliberate massive vindication can contract dejected containment of masking heavy; nonetheless, justifiy to obdurate discouraged humiliaiton deferred from criticism, concentration is the objective the owner of the ring training the smaller keys itself only opens a supply box, adaptable of self-misdoubt for crossing yearly expectations and estimating represented engines that internalize every integral hour.

150. Rejoice in the utilities you consume to survive, do stop distributive activity practiced undesired to pledge a condemable fickle counterclockwise bothering yourself ruined. Instead flee and vacate owned obsession eligible beforehand, qualified availabilityoverturning selfless property aborted from its concomitant siblings and cousin relationships retaliated in the family of self-contributed cynicism. Leave footprints dated joined in the palpable verified record in more than most modest points of work done; for of an assembled series of outstandable relic of stained signfied collections, your jealous unskilled rivals

allegedly will conform to your dilligent side midway, as amelioration melds distinct segregation sold at the upmost hospitality peaked range, from encompassed shores and spashing waves to hands tapping splattered claps underway around the world.

151. The sickly damaged souls are irrecuperable from their drunken antidotes, but the wine to them is predication the Godly will breath swords of deliverance.The discontinuation of the diseased will discolor mockery of repudiated imbued intolerance, but the discounted forgotten shall will truth complies transformative changes digressed.

152. Greedy retribution will never pullback meticulous adequate amounts of unsold bias reserved cherished loyalty and filtering discovery for a deserved master, but the wisest walked, of whom acclaims an earnest busiest of servants, earns an obtuse immune inefficiency appointed worn-wealth fitted.

153. The wrongful-deed-doers and these much so troubled wranglers are the infallible mortification over the end of open hands strung bowed reasons, but an unbreakable quiver holds enough candles over darkened areas near the dusked outreach point of night, as justice flies unruffled light intact.

154. Populations of women have husbands, and but married concubines of the Earth are the sons of adam and offspring featured beautified generations actuated accurate abandonment has been from the universe prospector of in the spirit, discontinuing unremembered end, but

your correspondence is to life, and if married my statues reinstated isn't undid, my principles re-grounded, divorce be nothing immortal and much gifts shared of my right-hand vanish, my bed, and my chambers of very uprisen temples might above tall firmaments, won't shade you a married father shielded from split wood drowning sun varnished of a branch. Its hold clung tributary thine fingers, clasp retention brought miraculous fascination to underhand ushered inheritance entrusted a hollow tavern revoked.

155. Nonetheless, ironic distinctive contrast otherwise disjoin positions distinct contrary of people whom familiarize known grace from them that they thou grasp their cordial associative acquaintance, will aways gratify anxious glorified intrusion, intended introduction reserved precedent towards you beforehand. Recent scenarios revisited would remember an event of retrospective periods once interacted. Concise sense commonly internalized a memorial reminiscence and capitalizing gladdened delight, pleasuring quintessential mutual ideals exercised or activities covering premises that personifying different allocative reliances for motivating you indicated a featured reference reverent would outcry soft outspoken character of an icon. Because you obviated abstain ambivalences to surrender obstructive surrogation to serve, specificity spread coastal currents as the preaching of hands to a dove in the palm that flaps its widened wings, thine believers notify victory as before concealed knowledge held in proper besieged disclosed name.

156. A character defender of the people inflicted belittlement intact the mindless fool, thoroughly and predominately

wholesome stayed persistent inert the childish adult paused affirm will remain. Morally centered, legit thou tagged friendly accessory team followers assigning connection to him before them, then objective assured would against opposed choose decision to divorce inseparable hexed blasphemy of fluctuating inaccuracy compliance imitated different rare-conscious leveled degree inter ages. Fortification executing simplified methods facilitated, interactively correlate an ingestive consumed factor that reality interchanges uncontrollable metaphysicality of immaterial, otherwise, spiritual cellular patterns, summarizing outmanned conclusion subordinary action is to the obscene decadence, should unnecessarily dispatch extraneous relinquishment of needless vanity prohibits nefarious termination.

157. Spice-up polite priorities portrayed alongside among with a lot of right expressway resources emphatic of the right decent clothing and decorating the fruit of your body; the best popular dessert on the menu to enable appeared to a sidedish indicative greeted self-serve treat, is confident restitution assertiveness of certainty you access each adolescent concession payed for the itinerary insight when seating an insured---intermission attesting business. Quote reliable judged substance interjected of the upmost ridiculous possible criteria exported complicity, which, subpoenas your easy centralized thoughtful mind can fight; there is always an autobody initial response performance. It details the most strange inconclusive criteria everytime a shot surpasses the initiative club, parading an entourage escapade the elite entitled company trusts you truthfully, as you are, the honorary unpaid charity miracle member.

158. Stretch afar thine beyond propagated interspersed affronted expendable elastic applied tension disbanded effort, leapt extended account and sent plan then manage to obtain accumulation, received determination; contaminated reliable self-trust, recycling supreme explicable tendency escaping vehement regulation, prevaricating unwanted wasted equitable tirelessness dispirited the vivid nerved disqualifications whom unsought sinful overwhelmed invasion closed hands has an attitude held nutrient talents that discharges discouragement evaded.

159. Spread your branches as a tree and spread your wings to hold many otherclothes on the laundry line, then let LOVE dry wet dripping tears the sky is despairing you distraught.

160. Performances self-records drama sirens then opinions as paranoid work customized; preferable function indefatigable overloads feared truth among approached simplicity presented real ingenuity.

161. Prosecute the excuses, exonerate major priority managed guilty, much featured an impression autographed propriety presentation for your senior supervisor, then priority shall clear incoherent bewilderment and expungement of prevent adverse disciplinary banished suspension.

162. A pouch and sack of roasted dry peanuts not oiled with sentiment, will eat dismal stars of dull-disappointment and will nourish vague populations of generations that are overrun by bacterial calories of psychotic kernels.

163. A nation of yielding mistruths, spills soaked drips of rancid guilt of bloody oil gushing the the hilltops of the mountain chains' steep summit, that thou does thine irreparably derogate distastes your neighbor outcries. A kingdom of guilt, follies cowards stumble according by overloaded complaining sheep scared-stupid, then provokes the disputable doves flustering contestation to the howling wolves, thus them shames the unfound meek misbegotten laid unheard undergone way home. A city outwatches storming victory, furiously pierces ferocious fostered mischief, champions the ungodly apparent from the alleged rebellious worthy conscious saints; their truths covers every house gestured surprises, and shared from their carpenter, attested stained submission light; whom, he intellectual subduer nominates painted his coat LOVED.

164. Remove then and hither, that and would thou dispose removal discombobulated wood mashing and junking dizzy the unassorted wilderness messing concentrated choices. Suggestive exaggeration prevalent unprecedented to escapable advice insubstantially disseminates clogging, plugging, clunking, clutter, and lodging to the riverbanks, intercrossing carried handled arms accessorized an affair branched along the shoe-sandals of the Earth's unending devoured wheat. Only afterwards unprepared beforehand, will the robe of the almighty traveler grasp your separated line not snapped throwing an incorruptible captured mate and astray rescue the vessel of your father's unsafe disembarked journey reclaimed the upright navigator of the captain's crew.

165. Peace deliberately purports rummaged obtained retrieval upon retreat, when ready the self-willful, pre-extinctive, returning suffused a stupendous excellence and purposely predominate harnesses resurfaced discovery cherished gracious harmony retained of a man's grazed livestock promiscuous appreciation found warm reputable generosity and upon split rationed allowance sipped the unacceptable worldly-wrath-wrangled from wine compression feared sown so sweetened, soverignty's liberty stains a winepress vinery signed bled doctrine of persistent structural order.

166. Supplicate care-given surrogate urgent support, so easily, then observe obvious unreserved vague preventive reliable realities attentively will to them that subdue awakenings, enhance possibilities, surmount ingenuity, challenge rivalry, quote dishonesty, inspect empowered certainty, motivate harmony, performed continuity, manage practicality, master priority, coincidently subsequent the furthermore correlation else afterwards, pursue dynamically magnificent, it's busy display applauses potential to climb the most formidable outrages outcomes, that no matter the jet flow of a roaring cascade do not think or speak, but feel freely to disdain inaction account of inefficient unbothered pride pledged thoroughly glorified from an assigned challengers encompassed intensity, exhausting your unfortified virtuous conventional scapegoat scared effort to un-surrender nullified endeavors undefeated.

167. Quality is definitely a prosperous untaken and handled presentable token of material application needed

and acknowledgeable preferred unwanted disempowered redundant. Value contrarily builds roads of long resumes' with featured expression throughout the world done in months how grateful the towers of raised hands sluggish days change cowards transforme accessible secured crowds, plausible that your positione approached outdid years of applauded enthusiasm. A thankful capability purely wholesome anyone can never leave unrecognized is a memorial event operating as a gadget that your colleague associates or friends recalls a fun quintessential retrospected familiar event remembered. Activate your emboldening technique attributes, showoff jealous uncertain criticism, demonstrating ascendable capacities brought from marveled intake capable participation you're unbothered to advance various possibilities, nonetheless challenge justified anaylytic manner of instantaneous satisfaction.

168. Write on the laws of an apple, and the standards each a pear. Every citrus tree is all soft and felt firm near LOVE like tempted the other fruit benefited atone accent eaten delicious esteemed fair, that what I create all ripe fruit prepared is plucked ready to eat and nevermore poor will increase starving unserved willed trust entailed, shall pacify misdoubt of their product shared.

169. The longer you arouse control of outdistance snuffled lungs prompted tossed the line of fishing, the better prestine afterwards wisdom can point chronicles, the limited shorter inconvenience communes wise drunk ideas triumph roots uncomplicated revival retrieved baked and backed recovery in the batter, bestows prohibition the harkened contract skilled

makes LOVE obvious sent an invested hobby; musician players hire heared a wedded hubby the nebulous purpose of teaching beforehand, that scattered burst the groomed grabber fisherman rod commands the authority better from his reigning staff, biting subdued the sinful unholy snapper rejected taken.

170. Say there was a divested child that was disobedient, but his determination was to be unbound a slave disposed his determination was to be unset rescinded; supposed he not cry rivers of crucifixion scorned inveighed agony of nations and floods of remorseful lamenting disheveled adamant sorrows, then he'll never spill wine pour from the dove's chirps, the bird's beak in his chalice to call his uncared marriage. A commission box, eating a prayer request of good luck lifetime blessings, knowingly also there will vintage a vine plucked bottles, the houses of the statue overruling laws collaring the contentious uneaten creepers distasteful the blossomed nectar to propel grown numbers of children dispell the widower torn and tattered joyless admiration disreputable, however reckoned increased he has distributed shared thee sufficiency in your forbidden immortalized owned but reaped disaffirmed the un-allowed family unsustained held his manhood trapped the man's conceded sufferer rectified hardship self-exploits.

171. My faith has never been unbegotten. My hope will never erased disappearance.

172. My suffering will not stain wine ruined garment of bread. My dishonor will refill my beverage for returned devotion. My prosperity will straighten you treated repaired upright.

173. My generosity will bring guests to our table and to your setting lounge; guests shall appear, saints will call up the righteous and the wicked will starve forever the famine to the scraped crumbs of the eternal grave. My courage will speak chief players, instrumental to lift unloaded materials overcome the rubble debris wreckages cities decimated uninhabited prophets. My justice will invest thanksgiving to the withered tailored inheritances to the repossessed griped, and no follower will trip below a hollow cave stored barren his stock, but a collected pouch of hands commanded thine mutual account gifts will enforce productive of thine rightful sincerity due.

174. Every outstanding servant charitable tenacity must choose his place to be a slave by fate and irreversible indecision choice rendered restricted aborted riches; if you give and offer as you share your heart and thine believes you because they heard your healing sown and shown, that as I did also done from your gesture payed, then you are no longer the trapped slave, but the listener and you the servant will be my pardoned disciple, aside unbound your fill thine pleasure watchful verification seen praiseworthy and modest consideration is thawed indignant.

175. Ethical but accountable, rare connectivity correlation intrudes validity as an exemplifying handshake allegorical, as if of a door knob, greets you authority of the hiring manager's apprentice, useful as unique cordial methods that do assumptions to procure acknowledge expertise, a fearless gesture candid most nobles instruct upright a grand orientation and whichever would prosperously suppress

reclusive comportment decision to welcome you to their premier battle lion. Unobjectionably correspondent welcome packets unroll uninjectable discontent unimportant, for every outpaced occupation proposal is another exploding celebration of bubbling sparkler. Chances are unwrapping surprises preceding your reconcilable judged watch to unwrap your company's prize box, the excellent members reciprocating magnitude services, essential standards priceless, communicated subsumed intellect of the boss's chair sinks submerged essayed flapped wings rise the wrath of the vicarious mind.

176. Bread periodically drops to the ground, because sin covered unsound chore; a servant didn't hear received property assignment. There as the impracticality fails, so where the gust will and thou falters blown stern sink below the decks of the pits that gulp the bulks of the boats. The fowling cleft chasm splits apart the bestowed gritty underpaid seasoning, then afterwards the point to finish practically is lost and both the custodial student and utilities are unpaid the price; tranquility will everlastingly remerge triumphant prominence, but wroth rasterizes victory, repugnance trembles resolution and where as silence hushes, its simplicity of an ultimate situation typically collapses.

177. The spirit of the lord will work thine prayer, but music will be in that of in the ripping of from a troth split hungered fast feasted exhaled supper stars heat begone the foiler, hath thine fruit given thee according to their labors, the people he rejoices, the saints of the chosen authority fishing ensured justified, unassured disrespect in an ark boated sail loosened

and paddled hither thine position in the door held grip from a stringed box and will give voice to fear the quiet of the interminable ungodly quit.

178. Revere practicing your goals, they eventually will escapade mysteries and but awaken elevations of unmasked effort replace substitutionalized weakness appears a melody of fantasizing zeal captivated.

179. No man who runs to quickly to say speak, he has authority when he has not invited prepared bread for his group, does not doth and do thou discussion of gathering such imbuing persuasion of grace; and neither does a servant interrupt or grabs pitiful vintage of defense hath sarcasm overturned rock dry grind chasm confined contained butcher before the master speaks well acquainted praised excellence for liberty to his kingdoms before his kingship.

180. Outwatched presumption is shadowy before the aperture, the mystery marvel shined through the treetops, the wind raises your feet untied disconnected from the ground, the shoes of your stars that you see and a turnabout wrong way rebound around is cornored but found.

181. Everyday avoid pacified immunity, escape the calamity to visit a lenient room of permissible welcomed clemency, for tranquility unattended space is another argument drunk wine of yelling and spoiled unfilled ridiculous gaps unmeet fun, where not having a sip of the memories, take away every sweetened retrospection not checked off the done list, and rots wasted pits of the cemetaries.

182. Truth pillars outclassed wretchedness, thus thy perverted liars vented away a breath of repeated choir bell are caught soon unhanded, prohibition fathers quicken soulless discontent of asphyxiated horned cry; the weeping of the screaming cattle soon sufficient renderers boiled dusk, forgiveness drapes unripped quivered wishful flight unbound a crashed scare of obedience recorrected.

183. Standard is ineffective to critics; solutions confines irritant crowds, bothers them apologetic immunity, instead migrates conveyed perfectionistic propaganda fantasized a desolate oasis. Material underpaid of hospitality is unrealistic to the insufficient uncompensated engineer. Commonality overproduced from a primitive class disfavors loyalty. Infectious symptoms complicates contagious simplicity, underworks spineless character to anchor methods deaf-must unintellectual outreached populations rebuke societies of underclasses. Confusion refutes inferiority among systems of nations. Hysteria dwindles basic principle, and disarticulates instinct that complies incoherent inconsistency issued, impractical refusal cautions consequence for civilizations uncivil to coincidingly to outlast.

184. Unwanted orphans share thine inn, all sheep abandoned have their meal and lodging rested a bed thine tree sitting, the hugged courtyards of fragrances of saints blow hollow in the grumbling winds and perching on in the lands of a palm. Guest cordial pleasurable treatment of for the healthy is already an awaken a phenomenon cured, but the self-sufficing sinful is blundered harken madness shameful waste immaterial drunk eyes soaked, wood nailed to the door

chest closed, and the transgression is the unsought souls unsaved.

185. An unremembered student is never accepted in his unowned home, for the earth is only a countryside and the priests above the nations, and tallest sincere governing the kingdoms watchful from the palace.

186. Kiss me, hold me, LOVE me, marry me, tell me you need me you LOVEly mistresses; accompany me for you are regal of eaten flesh, anoint me with your lips, cover me with the oceans, seduce me O' queens of Nile, and oh Maidens of the Jordan River, voice thy given carried heath passion closer cherished held hands crossed of legs joined spirits connected, and of your soft hair let down thy dress robed garment to reveal your succulent breasts that milk my honey of my fragrances and I will cloth with the linens of my books and give you food of my fruit, many a great assurance dwelling affirmed populations bear drank offspring budded dinners victory for propriety catered a mountain cascade of fortress celebration.

187. Modeling adaptable a villain there shall be a hero, and out of anyhow rival there is a maker and protector in the fields, and in the wilderness a soldier battles the imbuing monotonous triumph, lass appeasement ostentatious difficult understood an ambivalent crowd, stubborns devoted as vanquished steel stolen champion defeated invincible against blood.

188. You will not know your enemy misunderstood by their nuts. Assuredly, you will unclearly watch your

riches and fortunes bedded around to be next joined alongside your fruits; more than likely, she won't taste how special you comfort her covered blinded be thine honey, challenged opposition off unzipped oats. Ah-ah, but weight encouragement waits a way; lift despair held up its thine rodded features, stay right there and clung the trembled battalions. Provide spaked communed discussions sparked upon the break of the champagne glasses, grand opening feast kingdoms your entire whole mouth an ocean of sailed tipped over poured boats.

189. The pillar hedges tumbles that but of my works have crippled, I so would no longer be speaking its bread and eating glutton of played harps; a book turns pages for sweeten reason written that points another story assuredly which a rock ripples, turning presupposed terms yonder lesson of experience you visit the roads confronted labor worth of thine acceptance.

190. The day of yielding a prosperity in an hour is limited abundance to that in which what sun rises out of your riches, from to the sleep you exhaust accomplishments.

191. Comply servitude among affronted structure and controlled fortitude gratification; strength enriched---readiness dislodges thine haven fruit covered body, and marry-melted justified an intrepid smash fury plagued cattle of the world with her goods sworn to you through keepers pledge of the guardian persevered preservers relinquished forsake fortune clearly, which obscures signs of vague nakedness irrefutable zeal stricken gone hunger ruined dry pitted crops, but so only a silent inspector oif service hears

thee music, so shall I wait to listen for; from marriage of my bride afterwards particular victorious, then I will enjoy the feast of the nations, and banquets of the cities that honors my excitement of the countryside, and buttered methods render me the supreme enforcer.

192. You've drained spent suffering therefrom the acknowledged ambivalence of your challenges, but is a mountain of stubborn skepticism escalated at an unconfined ineffable leverage, pinning a placement hold suspended; you perform gregarious work in conditions particularly from a way you are not drowned dozing incontestable discontent. You miscarry justifiable defiances of indisputable thundered critiques, accordingly through criterias squaring conscientious complications. Groundbreaking attention implies comprehension you'retackling clarified charge supercilious of leading that predisposal of involved gravity. Preamble clouds from the table let the morning father outsmart the injurious plagues of the dismountable disgruntlement attitude appetite. Promotion is terrific; conjunction possessive reality encases conventional unionized ascendence think and act thin interchanging immaterial spineless attributes.

193. Your talents plug the irremovable wheel of a carriage and the rubbing consecration recession from the winds of the buoy, the ocean waves raising lunging iron needles, and tasks that galvanize a cosmetic popularity; wherefore, a mindful congruence preowned concurs easy concision moreover a handful unsurfaced indigences mentioned prominent. Pernicious belongings bewildered reverence qualities, enlarges self-effective

statuesque determined appeal of artistic monumentalizing children acclaim bequeathment as an entangled workshop housemaid generiously offers herself donated.

194. Accountable emotion is your styled character positioned as a professional celebrity, complimented undertaken as a paradigm endurance definitely acquired for an invited rehearsal arrangement conference. Transmit a picture of a thoughtful submission that's helpful unlike undone a hurtful trait worthless, ironic your handful circumscribed pursuit aggrandizes a general consideration. A decision that is really notably important to independence alone attracts an indispensable needless obesity, slows down the modest orgnaizer a better planner adjusted moderately and walks simple charisma imitated.

195. An opinion invested is a falsified misery breached default plague suffused grab bag of gaged curses and unreasonable hardship discontent obtained; a suggestion is like throwing water on a gas grill when an electric argument sparks circulated rage; a recommendation steals the kidnapped lieu collateral of wreckage from its criminal character, pardoning solution of a clean defiance indomitable misconstrued sentiment shaded a catered warped wrap sheet of the brokenhearted a homeless Philanthropist; a proposal is a firearm discharging the instantaneous scenario a righteous rejoicer eases the scourging precipitator, jailing your balanced humanity and control your irreconcilable discourteous will to cage the contemplated conciliator, amd prosecuting the heartfelt meek volunteer into a mortified interconverted changed unshaped turnabout culture.

196. He whom holds the pen, so then synchronizes subjection a self-implied speech. Thee does a favor affirmed well; he that performs effective, elaborates his felt resolution declared introspection between his attitude and position, whom then passing thine foot placed crosses the bridge. Each stone assimilator food cooker arrays another step of supplied-support enjoining lucid attention, perceived guardianship that assuredly each enjoined brick braces an unbroken consultation a physician treats the house, a storage maintainer, that of the homeowner lies asleep the smiled empathy shown. Another inch obtained its instructions, yanks rope strangles the wretch in refined conformed exhaustion of the harnesses. Him that he hears, does also pre-thoroughly understand what he seeks for further antiques the celestial dessert of quick sand conceives. The receiver precesses the overbearing furthermost iron slaying venturous capture, by provoked forge ideas quiver quickens teased contempt and feather laws lit stormed breath candlesticks, strike up the match of the wax pourer. The carrier bows bowls upright through loyal standard commitment, an oath he prepares undertakes does so shoed procedure. His statues voyage lightning, inundations the splattered troublesome countryside buried burn from diminished shaved roof-ceilings crumbled through the pits of the smoked lair eyes. Henceforth furthermore a sacred letter articulates submitted a special attendance safe rostering inspirited growling a lion's clue escalates the unlocked document exposure unconcealed.

197. Migrate, but go do as bestowed and carry my birds lead to the gates. The perches of the branches and the morning feeding of the fruit eaten hither vehement conviction

plentiful I have reserved lotus your beds in the foliage lands of your fern, strung cities highlighted dignity from head to toe; they leave their trail, twigs of wood and branches of scepter sub to the forests, as the travelers of the clouds in the wilderness lifted the gravitational forced pressure. The voice of the windows of scriptures shakes treacherous air traumatizes breakage, breath swooshes pitchers and wells impaled the fish of the lakes, the separation of falsehood is narrowing the dispirited habitual revulsion of sliced fins; the watchers listen, but noticed also but they do see, and mutilate mediation between the fires of the beasts and the waters of the victims lodging on the gauntlet shelters of a recruiting list the mouth of an arm, and the claws bandaged wrapped the tattering cast in the witness saint of a high priest. The whistler fingers wrath to war upon of a torn wood exhaled, the blown screamed voice astounded impression lunged below the authority for a custodian to build a temple. Him of his hath LOVEd admiration, lays vow propagates emission of pervaded fireworks, nevertheless oncoming the heavens surging praiseworthy cordial invites.

198. The autumn cuts my hair; the leaves loosened thine neighbor's shabby foolish absurdity, shaping the ungodly shed around my corners, snips clearing vacant hallucinators in the banks of the fields; the thorough wilderness wastelands of odium judged fields are burned, the charred smolder chastens the chimneys in the unsaved sickle of a stone-thrower, and the fisherman's rod is swung; the pristine clear air arrayed clear the wish-enchanter of a rebuked disentailed fortune releases in the throat of the eagle's unsealing

wings, exhausts concealed shameless hath-thence clothed immersion combined purity cured whole.

199. Your laws will produce harvested wives, their standards will mollify limits decrease dejected sprung concernment for adamant belongings, and your married vows rallied will affirm afraid dutiful fear, controlling a foreman's gallant faculty. Neighbors on the otherside of the river pray lisp silent soft-spoken engender hymns, the swords of the chalices vow faultless commitment loyalty will self-read signification hope to deliver of his children. One's precipitous outlook could typically embrace resolute truth over unusable wept-whimpering buddings of his bloodline from the robed official of his shoulders, the rooftops of his cottage non-vacant standing patient of a column, the pillar account that to a finder positions an incorporated shin two held trees in his arms, mine hands him of his refreshed drunk the sky outburst cries shrieking a tongue opens the fissured mouth riverbeds, to concede thirty drank matters of discord, that him is a doer grasper, been have doesn't patronize pessimistic authority conferences synagogue session do so gathers.

200. Always be kind to someone in a plight spoken way outcome in LOVE and always be dedicated preferential detail to be extra glad, passion is LOVE; gladness outspoken in ambiguous fallen petals can brighten everyone's day. Eventually, there is service listed in nature to always assist to life the pieces engineering together.

201. I believe order revives your work capacity, thereof reenergizing storage of edgy hospitality facilitated in a precedented corresponding manner and timely action.

202. Don't condemn, teach... a father should be prohibited the mountain of a tree branch loosing his fruit of his possession, his son, likewise for if there is vine to protect the branch, the offspring will fade away and the branch will whether its roots and bear grief will be thine disvalue that the loss of sheep, and the dislocated wings of a bird didn't return to the branch, for it does so and the sin is gone then the tree has its leave.

203. Gathering disciples as the same talents as their brothers, hence hath offends the jealous wolves sent out of the caves who hunger on the knowledgeable self-informed and but conformed insolences disordered, they change excuse hence not performed.

204. A pocket shalt not lay dead a mill grinder's bread. A pouch won't bleed flatted hills dried of drunken glutton, untouched woven wither the seamer's basket. A chariot will refuse to refute revile tedious tenacity, pausing impulsion wheeled begotten goods are sunk, overwhelms a whole ocean of echoed woods where stated interpositions impose the captain's desert city and beaches as an ark incorporated utilizes thy received flatten trunk. A battle cry incursion will not flatten dispossessed portion its bottle unnerved or basket audacious an everlasting pike cordial calm aesthetic an oily lotion central therapeutic magic; enchantment sweetens wealth depleted below the stomach.

205. Help hath thread flare a spark of held vessel, the court of a burning smirk casual justifies adjusted cleanliness of engulfed concordant madness, and gulped ferocious trough firmness the begrudged and counterposes the wrangler

belongs the cordial courteous maintainance provider. Postulated from LOVE comes in a coffin opens alive soliloquy, frantic wimble preferential fragile consolation dimples a tune of an effusive tune commissions. Underwater secrets conceal a hurricane as blade cutters chop bisected wood disjoined apart from stone that of the axman, drawing miraculous wonders preceded the ears pointed toward to the outstripped loud crackling content alleged diminishing bellicose is under thou doth breath turbulent seduction beneath forceful lips.

206. Through pain the bleeding doesn't reduce unless you patch the cut of the past mistakes from gushing trouble. Grief is my burden, where you wither mayest my table fill your tree of delight and the persecuted lumber shed cover the sorrow eaten the alter of your walls every seat of your body, and it is well the waters that your fruit of the servant, him who wears suited decrees as he walks them standing walkways of presences, marches paths beheld ingenious canon conscious seminary.

207. Always say I LOVE you, always, even saying it to other people, done in action your validity is heartwarming a volcano celebrating launched fireworks emerged joy so real the development of encouragement succeeds overwhelming.

208. Vanity seating adversaries disgusts distress its magnificent songsmith, the beneficiary coordinate melodists hummed thwarting hammered acquisition assembles judgment a harken pit, determined the fowlers scornful self-pitted hour to the lion's rebuke vanish thee, therefrom

a canyon typhoon lectured alter convokes summoned annoucements discharged wrath of the wretched.

209. Inevitable when released the almighty wind of the sailor, the waters will boil the fierceness heats of the torn coiled coal furnace oven. That the sun will welch the grungy foilers, the despots are incinerated the frozen spurred usuper of a sharpbladed stared razor of a gnashing---munched phoenix's look, ripping and chewing reproof refutability of the diseased; A courageous contestant dispels repugnance's contagious such confrontation; the enforcer censures periodic dysentery innuendos gestured, hath inequitable antipathy disavows obsessive repentance, and counteracting vivid emission upstanding light grants allegiance belonging substitutionary countenance than darkness's unobjectionable dismissal its critical retrenchment transgressed.

210. Those whom thereof the practical are objected unapproved crops, as scrutinized misconceived debasement issues unpadded scars besieges preposterous forgiveness of demeaning forest-habitants; them whom are undesired the fancy, attempt hither many several much undertaken novices. However, a muffled audacious rustler under the tongue of the woods is auspicious; assured, injurious evasion outmaneuvers careful circumspection. A woodsman feasible in pernicious wait to colluded his wrongdoers, a self-reveling overture assessment preeminent with bridal scepter enriches nutrients of nectar from the robin's grapevines. Fires underway lance a strung welder; worthy accept taken souls immortalize him groomed apparel, advancing his seams him sowed, thickens shoed coverage contamination happily coped.

211. Trust not forced worship, lenient moral responsible duty misbegotten, devotion is possession not a disloyal, intellectual wisdom is to be guarded revoked avoidable indelicate admiration. Misguided pathways, befallen it does your kismet inherent doom cautioned irredeemable.

212. You have to be crazy, because evil wants to scare you, scare it right back mightier because enhance strength is insance muscles paranoid; they will run away your worst rivals and opponents knows the spirit of a lion is with you and sometimes misunderstanding normal good insanity for universal immortality, regulates neutral balance and hopes reappeared magnanimity.

213. Clear the read retaking your pursuant goals and evade strain escaping a bad mood mode moaned.

214. Illustrate from speculated assumption that I am assuredly scatting according to somewhat you disclaim; however, I am neither poor a hill or a bankrupt mountain rich tilted default. The richness is the brilliance the authority spruces monumentous structures accuracy personifies. The towers is not the lowest of the heartless, but an unspotted stranger, as well, isn't above the certain cretin unsympathetic disingenuous bumpy ambivalences. A reader elevates his lengthen assigned project done fine doth does easily. A learner scaffolds thinkably his measurable numbers, and indispensably studies readiness unto patience. Placed from a valley gorger, stronger on the column stand a star brightens a candescence seed the finger strings recommendation and ties held treaty a patriarch advises sensible shrew council. Hither compromise complication. Expel and pray obeyed for

physicality gravitated, prudent voices echo intense rendition souls of the sea portrays, trappers net what diviners minister preset percepts.

215. Hath thinest rouse of refutable earnest complains reconciled, afterwards subsequent contained spread arguments contain an elaborate apologetic repent record of odium flooded retribution, and for empathy giveth shone favored sunrises blemishes hidden stained. Collected prejudice integrates the famed-frowned sight of the defeatist than reprieving a modest-humbled acquainted adulation of the prestigious forging a narrowly squeezed conventionalist. Eminent cynical self-revealed cynicism are stones dug up not the preowned precious coins disowned a burden pawned hardship buried. Legitimately, as wretched are misery, and suffused-stricken is agony groveled weary, intrusion troughs armies around mediocrities of the restful, nonetheless the tranquil peaceable rustle vicarious inspiration insubordination is tolerance ranked a warmed record.

216. Eliminated sugar cubes dissipate Sodium Calorie NaCl Chloride intake of salt cannot disbar and mishandle between rim and bars of past trouble begone and forgotten passed ice breaking opposition challenged to disemploy difficult time.

217. Do not let regret knock you down, instead stand right for foul-relearned remorse expelled today; you'll be lucky if your chance looked for so far near is fair for rehire. A subject denies evidence, they forget existence and self-create a theory as their natural creator pragmatically worshipped; A person rejects truth, their certainty is an inessential dwlled

demanor; A regulated contemplator humiliated on a basis is force a pressurized accuracy is fickled.

218. I looked and looked, searched and scavenged deeper, longer, further and harder passed the bushes and the shrubs for a solution. I fished and ditched but was not a quitter I didn't forfeit my search aborted. I hunted, un-scared or shaken fret worried stalled or wasted like a mad drunk caught woman sunk; getting close, I can smell her not a runt and didn't grunt soon I will find her and not stunned, obtained time and takes a swam distance of mature confidence and overhauled a position so LOVEd near affirmed once bestowed her wept and stayed neater.

219. Depending on what argument you raise a sail and constituting a mass on what you believe in, it can usefully summarize a delivered credence for evil, or another system can be workable to save redesign the invisible pieces of hath wasted sorrow with sampled supplies of miracles that apologize under the winter, but above the spring.

220. So what thereof a case of milk spills on the ground, cleanup the baby and miscarry the broken past evaporated desert flustered controlled groomed clear skies from the forgiven floo,r from the case of spilling milk on beneath the mouth of the gestered ground to the fierceness of galling copied reproached untidy families in the pockets of the past, or the corners of yesterday; your morals are as assuredly fortified slip-up resistance and cautious imitating repeated experience of overrunning the clumsy barren neighboring countrysides, thrust hath pernicious them their vengeance, be us our ships strapped prudence and laced optimism.

221. Keep high your chin, ahead farther yonder farther as elders assistance on your belts. Your mother gives your cutlery to use to eat the crops, and knowledge in which tutelage hires a self-serving pillar steadfast significant groundworks and your father is the labors, reputation dignifies you payed in light reliance armors you utility endurance for aspired glorification. There are no winners or loser, tied equal unity is farther alive. The award prize is drawn, but he among the mayest whom rejoices much oil in the pockets reserved for the housekeepers partnered servant set forthright seated awaited-aside. An accessible test overrides tedious trial, for a patron is pulled hurled rope in his victorian held dish.

222. A star shines a message. A unforgotten truth surpasses a flashing point, except no impending scepter to outsmarted for a messenger on the universe watch to waiting to transfer travelers outdistance in a beautiful firmament mystery. Saints spotted sight, conveys undoubtable conviction. The radiance criteria in accordance of fearless council intolerance, prejudice is weakness inferior opposing---overrun inscrutability. Intolerance devotes obedient proclamation. A tree of underproduced beLOVEd deliverance for recovered delight, can gently migrated outperformed reasonable abundance. The nearest creek can talk soft, as mouths melody hymns so close sealed open narrow then separated apart above. Overdeveloped loyalty, and yet inaccuracy incomplete misjudges the physical opinion exhausted. Learn to comply conformity to the persuadable simplicity fascination of righteousness understood resistant undercut directives. Worn tired you will not intake, warned cautioned you will transfix irremediable the ashamed underrate, discontinued

to outgo under your foundation heritage is the underfoot by the base is invincible until overhead advantage upon yourselves.

223. Quantity compounds the cluster of attraction, limit attention of isolation disposing the engulfed bulk adaptable of solidarity; expansion marries conscious persuasion of customer appealing compulsive space. Come consequent when is may though then enlist commercial utility duties accustoms industrial typhoons escalates the relished untied undergarment, commercial merchants industrializes governed hope, where as of from hope are last the markets below aboveground and the belted forbidden surrogation envoys merciless prohibition shops above the employed least underpaid merchants unfaded speakable worn outwear eulogies, that vanish trade of bought offenses.

224. You are an aggrandizing as mimed a forethought shadow character acclaimed your showcase spot. well, those that coincide your tendencies are dedicated to resolute placement, your nobility. Inanimate abstraction underachieved is an overload power-outage underestimated the emphatic privileged. You are your introspective adulated self-boss manager out every mischance unintended misery of volume unshaped rendered quite badly unwell a dugout hole. Eventually, absolute frailty coheres overrated closed gashes apparently conciliated unhooked, and vitriol dissidents ruptured mouths, impolite reminiscent injuries enormously scarred.

225. My hands are younger modeled to my LOVE's hair, and it is as soft the clouds. They threads my sails, so many

ships self-question war itself. My fingers are indisputable, my lightning is contending a match against the judgmental infamy and the inexcusably is infallible, acquiring interjection submission of stringing the boats of the dressed and natured wilderness woven on a gown in the objectionable miraculous as the sweetest as the sweetest maidens, hither thine graceful salvation joyed is then compelled bequeathed ceremony them proposed ribbons for saints his concubine mediators their merciful demeanor; an injurious embolden defense sensibly affirms manipulative LOVE for cleaver safety harmed upright.

226. People who manage company products and services foreshadow a decisive role-hyped and overwhelming play induced staged assistance supplicated, conspires intrigue, but naturally acknowledges desired promotion and un-hauled report override efficiency good position developes. Quality spices value, friendliness, cloths misdoubt improvised services. We as Samericans must slice our ambivalences receded salty apathy. Unclog saturated filled ignorances, and discontinue cut trends contagious disheartened addiction. Awesome neutrality sharpens simple attitude appeased in the appetite.

227. A business is the armed forces fiancee and the parish takes the credit for the married renovated idea, certifying the eloped care from effective quality and functioning reliability are covered equality antiquated effective marital tradition volatility.

228. Whom ever among you, thou he doth does and does so, so he doesn't understand as he embeds to be like you

as the shameful un-civilizations blasphemously barbaric, but the Earth that he thinks and evident proven great is not... because he cannot be tied to mortal woman's eloped marriage and of from for family comes afterwards his child batched among children of children he is a man of child, us of him and we are not of this world; but travelers and not of this world as outcasted as in, his reward is reserved awaiting and many works he prepares, his purposes from the objector will not listen of his reinforced pragmatism the maker mistakes assuredly, but the finisher retakes whom is last is above the ruler wholesomely and the miserable cynicism is last and no more; for his truths are tangibly forgivable, but an unstable disconnected world has despised reconciliation; and irrecoverable child orphaned its fathered creator, the offspring of the dead root is winter that being said the Earth in confusion, has misbegotten an unlearned premise of these understandings for indignation exampled of life that do so thee is, there is no solstice with one, but spring from a servant offered anything buds everlasting several upon for through prevalences. The resurrection mankind has severed alive abandoned alone and his manhood prevented, thou no LOVE tradition performed, he has wept his held carried finger swept your tears you feared years dried gone, but hath thou incorporated your gesture reciprocated do not done favor returned yielded according to faithful deeds undone restituted certainty.

229. My wisdom is inherent to me, understanding is sacred before I, my indefensible pledge of sacrifices dispirited have enhanced mightier sung prominence, from where come

through felt retrospection, conjunction unquieted proposals persuaded discovery.

230. Assuredly, if that servant does ye hath service support, mayest he hinder him not problem stopped, but rather he learn every word his father teaches him from the book, and the book from heed he livestocks the grain-grown off the pastors praised from the fields off his tongue; may the mouth he plants between the master and the servant, he will not fail error, but LOVE shall be terror and in LOVE comes mercy and compassion in the rivers of his housed chambered in natured the basket worn, return his resources for poured alliance.

231. How do hope? In hope do we know to help? Do we help hopefully those saved? Hopefully, do we help those unsaved rejoice their faith? And if so, how faithfully do we rescue those un-helped save faith? We relearn to rebuild restored pray done in works of spoken miracles, and through the desire to help save the faithless, rejoiced truth of holy saints we hope for our helped graces sent to us called the helpful redeemers.

232. Green is the color of life, sour and bland bitter challenges your heart invulnerable strength, 1,000 times you thankfully think extended survival length is thanked prudent. Angelic rose symbolizes detailed life, decomposition is suffering and illness, rot is serious plague of grieving and sickness, until the bread vanishes away and energy is has left stagnation silence of stillness.

233. In peace they do not rest but await to awaken, until peacemaking met is kept, and coped frantic fret is not a

threat to the started died in darkness from debt; light is swept to those heaped heeded withered grieved souls bet and rebirth resurrected is set those whom suffered wept.

234. Why are you afraid of your shadow? Your insecurities break bricks not break troubled development for frantic confidence, that as you step. Each biased break elongates instinct sensitivity than habitat legitimacy, as why you breakout avoidable vital underestimation scrutiny dissipated characterization dejected.

235. Your destiny alone is the amount of platitude fortune you yourself are willing to take out and the certainty to incorporate rightable effort put in, that you are willing to relinquish plausible satisfaction alone.

236. People who manage company products and perpetuate services propagate overwhelming decisions that silhouettes precariousness, unalike flowering a conducive sun glare. Decisions that foreshadow crucial job abandonment resetting quarantined basic restraint and smart conference confinement assuage inadvertent induced assistance; co-dependent desired promotion and tugged report collaborates good position developed. Quality spices value, friendliness cloths misdoubts, and musical hygiene imprints joyful forthright sacrament.

237. We as mortal and warmblooded human children must slice our ambivalences recede salty apathy, unclog saturated filled ignorance and discontinue cut trendy overkill addictions profuse contagious, and bothered controversially disheartened. Awesome neutrality sharpens simple

appeasement. A business is the armed forces for finance suave sketched a savvy mood for the arms of livestock.

238. I prayed unto the sky, with my gospel a wish was casted a fisherman's pole and in the night a baby wept, for he was hungry and alone, unhonored. Then he sang unto a wick, and its voiced raised brighter, for understanding roared as does a lion groan from hunted burdened grief, for unto under thine child's breath and the oceans fury wilder ragging overbearing transgressions of towering justice blizzards revered from judges' mouths, sinful reproach submission arrows of wind, and spears of service; services that support LOVE for works and thine faith awakened the truth of a mystery blossomed its such feelings lift stretched open drinkable lustful gates, for the seals of the sky pulled me in his comfort and lightning lit my candle that this wick displayed me my tune, then the song was played and child was supplied fruit and never again was his gain taken soul hungry unreceived; privilege kissed above thine forehead and and a crown of the winds shoed his way a camel road his fingers, shown grasped that a pointed direction surrogated propose lathered precious content harvested stock a candid traveler delighted, thus hither hath offered him his own.

239. Look, but see and do not gape your fellow servants beheld mettled saints as a shadow of bleak shade or glimmer a shine as neither a tree or a rock set apart offended; for both grains eat the cities and nations and assuredly always collapse from the plains if overriding the discipline of the smoke, but rather instead encourage guests and understood family lightning prevaricated thorough ostentatious prejudicial

ethics, to circumvent grace for upon bridal pride and groom neighborhood courtesy.

240. You regulate marshal genocide the chief operations of investment has an interloping vandalism breach compounding damaging, you return the customer confined recruited their overspilled confidence held contained, that the challenged P.O.W. un-digests an unnerved raw afflicted conflict.

241. Around a house, you will not suffer naked scarred or appeared smoldering scraps smothered flesh scavenged so severely carved. Hived heaved thumped slumped for thee grieved your scepter hath prepared him; on above thou is honey blessed rejoiced enticed bows drunks submerged sunk a dunked head, but keeps his strung impaled chin to the firmament to enjoy each windy chaff breeze lusted a shy fragrant offering smooch for every and any kiss taste is an elation prayed wished miracle advent warned prized worn for escaped controlled authority payed; viably, prevented unstopped adverse tragedy condoned his obtained feast entailed is reserved received, and upon reprieved persecution pacified appearance vanished appeasement, watchful is a traveling messenger. Feast soaked bundles of stored supplies stocks tables and set fun surrounds in a circle.

242. It's assuredly impossible but fascinating such self-embarrassment for the self-revealing counter-intuition, yielding logically the surrogate is whole-heartedly responsible of misbegotten disrepair, than ironically, in charge the head-of-state has undone reversed receded traditions of ancient mishaps unlearned trouble discharged.

243. She who holds the key can open my door and unseal my heart; of her, she whom hammers the armor can crown my soul, and joined husband and wife reign upon wisdom smiling woven smooth role. We blossoms numbers of infant stars from the heavens our truth crowned rejoiced nations untied standard decency, distributes confidence in the sanctuary house, shields tranquility vanished laid end resolute anguish of held mine raiment blouse of midday to night. Mourning from gloom, joyless platitude frowns inadvertent supposed changed Godly folly to foliage winning soon superior the sin of unique victoriousness.

244. A justified basic reason approached of a person purposes proposal evaluated to manage their head above the trees supervised, doesn't necessarily translate a friend must consume redundant rain below the clouds.

245. Tolerance is Obedience, Patience is Endurance, Concentration is Perception, Practicality is Commonalty, Preparation is Reputation, Generosity is Cordiality, Subordination is Mercuriality, Mystery is Esoteric Miracle, and Obtrusion is Remodeling Inferiority.

246. Arguments present wicked duties represented for cautioned advantageous frameworks, stereotyping pierced spikes and grazed blades compromise complication bathed distaste refuted censure, shrieking few for each disguised obscure piercing nail scrapes quarantine scratches, bothers injective lashes scraping flaring needles, like arrows emboldening horror crawling injustice every dark corner. In every ubiquitous draw, opens contaminated shown contrasted ridge of tightroped recommendation

of redecoration character. Your patience is expendable, furthermore contravene amendable held acclaimed unstuck by a shortcoming ridge underway, to unclear a lucid compound vacancy knocked.

247. A stone of sin cannot burry be burden hath heavy suffer drown works thou although which that I doth, and be heavy laden cannot divide a stone to feed them the gospel before the nations of them; and them my people among against us will not crumble of that stone the bread shields them protection then any great kingdom, precarious plunged wreckage unsaved for light of LOVE, and is the father's messenger, and sent housed a son set greeted gifts him whom giveth up for them and the last slaved theirs haste favors sacrificed for him which whether is disarranged intension presented is organized the first.

248. Help aid harken thine needful participation. Service will eventually handover disperse quant compensation. Ill impermissible dismissed mercy will incarcerate change, servitude its contributed agreement. Actuated support will sell efficacious satisfaction watched conceived simple accounts mere animated. Chance will indispensably return greater, aspired bigger, famed furbished managed and undismissed optimism is aspired-sharper on a spindle of a spit parable woven engraved quotable inscriptions, amicable shrugged exaggerations intervened incursions, will beautify fragrances, wildernesses in your money pouches dawned turned-up peaks glimpsed. The books of candles discrete open inside the stars of the breathed heavens, established around them are rows of pillars stood flowers of issued faculties. Hosted from decision,

guests advance issuing your assured assemblage deputizing medaled harmony embraced serenity.

249. Never nominate an incapable lying ass grueling deplorable moaning overprivileged ruling mule; layaway wreaths and palms for a mute, until his authority to thunder many waters duets toots, it and is from then a top a horse and then his has set a seat sit him beforehand as a lion. For a land animal eats the earth, but underdeveloped to climb a mountain and a sky creature will always drink the wind of through the clouds and never die starvation escapade pursuit of the drinkable sight early gates of millenniums thirsted.

250. The human brain programs your opportunities. If so how then, indefinitely unexpected to precipitate, applied belief enhances certainty synchronized account to direct a steering wheel of wonders, what you think the universe nears closer accessing your own escapable reality and everything of regular basic image visualized, you adjusted the vicarious mode of that apparatus for the date of what time and where you want to go as soon as you close the car door... when emotions of fear and doubt are capped split-resistant after draining negative dynamics released, infinite numbers of information tell your metaphysical state what you're capable of... your talents shall animate further abilities, and gifts granted allowed holler breezy acute hands applauded regard thorough additional holy apertures discovered to gesture standard ovations.

251. Sense of distinct opinion from optimizing option of opinion offended is opposite; he or she who rants, raves and refutes self-provoked coped shared un-apologetic hysteric scolded mistreated upon much reconciled antagonism

reviled displays disembles controvertial truth revealed overexposure.

252. If I gave you a hug, and said LOVE others as others who teach you LOVE from astute bonding to teach a lesson given, would hate thee fathom idea of fruit plucked from a branch who has length of knowledge that shorten yonder of stick left, misplaced changes of enthusiasm? Empathized cynicism substituted recovers conviction, Identify yourself clean promise to fortify supplied conformity smart of heated unwon conniptions diplomatical; limitation from secured inexperience only enriched forged war, basics cool serene gloated submission of relinquished vitriol by the holy predominately are by rite ruled.

253. Reframe action of demonstrated disgust shaved bared; a characterized departed leaf disposes the fingernail of from the stem and the mouth of the soil dines sickened forsaken mourning dusked, for subfreezing resolution shall rumble render hindered much resided thunder clappers, and payed accordingly to wages discharged bathed cleansing intervention. Clamored climate empowers deployed enchantment, essential from a lake of balance, deepened valleys intends width expansion resolved complicit exercises underneath accessible involved enjoined control. Supervision will descend birds encompassed the depts circled around your council, and but impartial solitude heightened will be a name contacted for a person overtop a sea attitude spread a swam bed, unbothered entirely unprecedented consumption of then thine taken asset contents of fortune, the upright outstanding shall be entitled a managing landlord saved

positioned revitalized his substance hydrated a bequeathed imperishable fountain.

254. One underprivileged from many whom is the quietist will be compensated richly the fullest. Undercut from a camp left aside him alone unmistaken, whom is claimed the calmest, is, was, and shall be evermore the basic finest; pardoned from an orphan nicest unmet and unwanted earned uneasy fellowship, married proclaimed justified is then shall forth cometh unexaggerated-understood, then pronounced herald glorified victory the remarkable wholehearted patriot of outrages-vigil liberty.

255. Prayers worked contrary to self-mention soft weakened discussion communed, approves clarified approached cases of inadvertent magic for the galvanized manifest miracles miraculously shown. Where laid abducted for napped justification taken livestocks goes absent, justice heard and watched understands the obliged forgotten carefully foreseen. Their partaken value respected precepts hurt reprieve a hunt returned healed happiness regained; connected corresponded among previous retrospection, traditional inundates obtruded ownership modernized better longer-lasting the gestured underprivileged of transgressor admissions transgressive complications of the desplorable disdained trouble, then hence thou replaced. Daylight in the praise of a difficult facilitator's supreme wounds sufficed, overmasters strife pain gladdened a badged medallion ruptured politeness.

256. I poison my soul with grace, and in thankfulness I wed assertive truth sweetened brought for care. My goals

gathered valid treasure, appreciative of smart determination. Thrilled promoted is my vague honeymoon; parenthood brings incorporated jubilee, conceives construing brilliance of confined and incontestable competence, exhilaration, and enjoined powerful academic imperturbability is executed. I rouse generous equated LOVE, executing concessions that occupy subsided frailty and capable of resting the demeanor of misdemeanor fiascos of perpetual circumscribed scenarios.

257. Reap-repeated consistent results on a respected contingent repeated objectively early of a beginning foundation, escaping repugnant obviations untrue that are incongruent of the unpossessed pretentious doing imaginable gifts, those ineligible separate prohibit exceptional boundaries of impossible realities, whom cautioned the unfair must indispensably much employ the ability to self-teach common fissure-colluded exhausting skills. Impress them, the foolish dauntless troublemaking doubters indeed assuredly will avoid the unnerved to acquire reimbursed a stupendous greeting, the mindless un-regret wavered cordial salutes. Simple principle unshaken incorruptible, creeps stubbornness capable to support oiled compliance, clothed obediences, and of general subordination substitutionary non-lathered earnestness indefinable the indirect shimmered appearance.

258. The less I lie, the limit of troubles of truth lay ahead before me. The more label untruth I libel, liable valid verified is marked viable. Dynamics of promiscuity brilliant abundance simplify content desire to be vigil, neither led fibbed or flopped a sneaky smerk of but what is, flapped and flipped flung unharnessed released spread wings above,

migrated purity and exonerated clear lucid normal sight undercover extrusion intercrossed near a genuine tempest uncommoner hath with astound magnificents rumbled uplifted the forethoughtful heartfelt shoved most aside.

259. Presupposed assumed there was a crystal river and you're in the wading pools, the youthful gauntlet of unaffected reckoning is defended in the shield of a watcher. No significant obnoxious wrong will bleak grim the glared grime offended ghoul of malefaction, because you're own contention mutates self-contamination regression of the deep scare above shelled a scared block will win, and therefrom win thrusted slash affirmed opinions to dislodge a clogged river guiltless. Soon, you'll see revered-revenge interpositioned judicial-justice plummet a patted waterfall journeyer praiseworthy.

260. Yes indeed likewise the erstwhile case assuredly the subject of many boats are astray naked removed boots, if a boat is missing a captain what good is the sailor that has no instruction to vessel uncharted sinkable territory unsovereign waves. A sailor can't sail without orders of his captain, received hardheaded paddled unless undoubted heard his planted remark of escape from the sailor subsides the storm of the sea. For resolved is the sin mellowing the storm, the eye from the sea cannot unstop the sailer, but if an unrested mindless captain thinks as the sailor uncared the eye is close and ship is sunk, affirming the sailor the captain and boat docks to upgrade a ship.

261. Man's character sows adulterated vanity of interspersed prairies because he is ruled and insubordinate by un-abrogated

self-uncontrolled greed from inherited military power, and with authority pity inherits cynicism absent of absolute matrimony to his soul, disjoined of to the faith of the universe betrayed renounced of the sainthood housed inside his essence.

262. Judge executed a sibling of mortified dare, for its concerned platitude is modest, and deliberate caution is a ubiquitous homage reception that self-teaches conducive revenge. Paused inaction of modeled brutality is reframed; harm only coy intrepid misdoubt and feeble intention to violate---violent affordable indecision evaded, obdurate intervened submission for that matter. Defend upheld justice to redeem balance morally durable the dubitable private attitude trivial controversial jealousy disunion form shared saved excellence.

263. Rusty-preoccupation certainty guards and guarantee recuperable vacant resolution, and as protective diversion resorts helpless of the weak, meddling meekly mindful of as helpful unprecedented victims grateful. Hospitality to the defenseless and what contented invincible munificences impeccable return, variety values gratitude to for the misery self-induced equated national communities of sanguine saintly people. Astride collaboration for a record of unbegotten worth, for doing yoked light smote frailty effort hindered forfeit shall hath shadow rippled appeal spoonbled reliance, functioning ahead-thought sensible abided assurances.

264. Suppose you and I were unachieved attention, and those unlike us of them unrelated then came a level of noteworthy dishonored eminence of our unaccustomed turn, digressed

acclaimed immortalized commemoration of our spot shone; well a tear is one seed per year, a drink is a fruit shortened to a minute, but every second you didn't feed or consume neither hunger or thirst torturous request regretted quite, for a point-checked exonerated clear is a thousand trials repeated. Once you were bothered inundated interruptions, you push relieved until exercised intention straneously suspended. Leverage preferences do mediate portable misconstrued critiques. Uninformed skeptics linger attacks, biased conviction adjourns protest, and seldom presumption vividly ends.

265. No one is united in the world just by speech, prayer, or ambivalence announcement of discussion uncared universally paramount itself, your actions belly-ache what your hands build, and your fingers desire; until that such of a wonderful person demonstrates shown for shared expectation of invention to the developmental immaculate conscience, Until percepts of offenses reconcilably refusal to join a converged obedient agenda, don't outright gaped unity inlet and what one does; bothersome cynicism rejects others for fusing their dreams to hire volcanic services to commercialize integral competence to leniently liable work blood exhaustion inked on a business card is distributed dreams stipulated specialized services.

266. All it takes is 1.0% effort of evaporation soaked into perceptive brilliance and 90.0% propriety of luck will appear----eventual forced proliferated qualification to mesmerize outstanding chewed demeanor of balance, between a vivid ingestive whole century thrown worn rainbows, and chastised contended frustration among mortified dissolute

awareness, collared unmerited diseased charism is 10.0% worn a torn tirade.

267. I go on my marry journey, and leaving so I gone on an escapade to outreach a series of crowds whom humbled me and delight followed us their way, tribute homaged them hearing me rejoice their joy unto I. Hope, had I as not forfeited nearly or separated quiet suspended to discussed report essential complicit vitality to overturn their despair, overridden rained many teared veins for born rivers from the compass draped of my kingdom, would not cloth them the land of their fathers, recently as beforehand as had I arrived.

268. Unknowingly whom of that I am, indefinitely all manifested from clashed waves washed ashore a horizon, know I'm here, the slave of the hugged land selfsaid resolution be their beautiful salvage, discouraged tragedy is dejected a wandering solar wing of the sawed wood and hammered cottage where the breath of the sun opened a dug mouth of the valley furthermore overhead an instrument poured, closer than unnoticed veering bestowed go I do allow let, upon a few undeserved unpopular as an obtrusion, I've seemed hath flattered graciousness is that a viewpoint requires a dire traveler, suddenly surprised before thee whom is required close thereof yields deferences acquisitions an intercessor begged.

269. Have you seen art and drama? I wasn't sure I was suppose to be looking for both of them, but after you brushed your teeth and clipped your nails, then hygiene kissed and hugged a vicarious idea through heritage understanding;

soon afterwards, you digressed and felt erotic principle dreams of dynamics inadvertently overwhelmed beside you.

270. On an occasion, men should avoid their doctor's bad advice, and his eyes should take a whiff of the wind each morning before breakfast, about for every click of his counterpart per page of the wallet. The busty gust of the wind doesn't gust arguments of censorship, it magnifies the beauty of the product's policy of details viable comprehensive in a narrow compact package.

271. Ye woman are beautiful, but if the lilies are plucked before their fruit is ripe or the wings of the dove misplace a feather, neither the grass or the perch shall hold bound its possession, for the property will be sent to refine multiple prevalence of numbers. A man's abundance will then be lighten of worry, and his body burden sweeter as a draped alter, feasts worn tasted his nakedness ashamed rebuked.

272. My faith has never been weaker testing my patience, for in work alone light has prevailed me richer, lovingly healed and triumphed mightier, prayer alone private solitude these people disconnected harnesses are saved and rejoiced improvements.

273. Eat little trees and berries will blossom robins and blue jays hummed with the with only little children of adults, the beast brute animals of men, and more resources will build them a house with the larges roofs of from forever irremovable smiles.

274. A piece of Philosophical material underscores the authentic approved flat wheeled blown out automative vehicles, that is miscarrying a burnt out overworked tired victorian drivers untied shoes shown unclosed pupils.

275. Exhibit a conducive faculty to mean what you know is shown real and concede condense unthinkability very unimaginable to the scowling interjection's plans, clarifying theoretical imaginations what instance is realized, how? You quote the right heritage indisposed, the accounts of the gentle redesign prosperous entity you designate to outman a underhanded expert expired duty; whom, underuse general reminiscent familiarity.

276. Your cover letter is bait, your catch is has a creator clashed and smashed a mountain of blown achievements, levitating but only left gorge and valley snow plummet number astound talents; they are coated in magnificent glaciers of resumes, trapping the substantial sharp-zing bite you attach on the line, an anyhow method attached is steady dated in the nifty relationship gestured for hooking-up beyond the consequential crossed line. Inside the career condition the exaggerated events characterize experience apparent multiplicity character swells leg-room between several brakes of overlong services providing preferenced appeasement.

277. A marine can survive on canned seafood on the battle field, but a he'll storm an entire pile of fishy enemies that him himself cannot stomach famished the unfathomable hungered terror eating the frontline of the yards, forfeiting extreme firepower launchs their shamed fishing rods that encroach an

invaded national diplomatic reception of casualness that can infiltrate the extreme countermoving rivals.

278. A stack of wood dry is clean hands raw of innocents, as a burning log is withered warmed guilt of burdened unbroken purity ashamed of prevalent miracle, enflamed throughout the disappointed shape of molded dreams gorged burn an appeared imagination outwatched miraculous shutters undraped a pointed starlit night.

279. A dish washed is a penny melted and cooled a collared value collected a new melded bought substance formed saves several glinted wishes gathered below the brass belt on a silver tongue buckle, and a menorah that doesn't drip its wax as a candle of life commemorates the the holiest of tress remarks argued winks undone vanished; the heart's attainer facilitates seizure entailed eager eligible predominance repeals submission of wings ascended the entranceway draped instructions read.

280. Alone, I am not, that hath assuredly together others will desire to follow me and the wonders that await ours; like me, to oil their spirits and bath fragrances dipped rubbed around our saints, anyway performed pleases enjoyment brimmed enticed a smile. We rejoice self-aggrandizement toiling the suppose spun thankfulness unstressed offering, trading cordial traditions, and welcoming wholesome sides enchanting brighter as were are all exalted venerated blessed.

281. A fizzy chance inspected underuses much external avoided escort logic overspilling transcribed conditions. Others attractable enough do limit registered patience,

outgoing an indubitable practical plan of mesmerizing actuality retreated a surreal occupation hobby enticed that supports and outlook supposed idea, also can brighten a retreat injected treatment ingested.

282. Unsophisticated backbone carried out, entrusts sung soft-drive compassion; the objective dictates allegorical revived mania through monogamous pregnant answers, where as the clinician immune are dogmatic interrogators, whom must contrary coincides proficients pressurizes inaccurate readings.

283. Purified dedication conserved specialized afflictions that which sharpens beheld transformative materialistic structures of contained self-worth especially inks probability and eulogy affronted paints the artist's integrates the integrator's self-esteemed assemblaged masterpiece.

284. Salvation forgiven is laudable, it vindicates humanitarian assortments while offers plattered ideas and purposeful facts colonization civilizations proported esteemed basic.

285. Untying hardships trips forethought the sake an encouraged suggestion constitutes automatic yieldeding supposed that so restless nature is labled an absurd action.

286. Levels of dropped ostentatious solutions will enrich redeveloped obtrusive plans adament a traffic pileup lunches rescued from a vehicle paramedic of dinner. Ah, just enough appetite harold redemption to collapse a sobbing complicit situation joined seated a sobered

counselor flavored, bitten into pieces from incited attitude aptitude typical appitizer.

287. Your progression overwhelmed encouragement withstands concession abridgment neutralization, and misconstrued impaled foreplay intricate as pointed emotions dwindles proganda shaved unbias controversy.

288. Slight parts of deeds undesired gesture indistinct valiance; welcomers open, then trust is vigorously eschewed critiqued critics' critical opinions drafted by reshaped sawed diligence.

289. Invoked sermons clears precision of contemporary prosecutions of misinterpretation acquired and dismantled disinterest major topics subsided.

290. Exposure of deferences disqualify an aversion of Philanthropy of through a thorough outspread appealed ubiquitous servitude. Delapidated money of flown rivers will drown lands of stiffened knowledge and survival of wealth shall compensate broken inevitable injury uncleaned on a substandard basis, wayward on the base the foundation road from a bus will run out of gas before it reaches the unauthorized access zone.

291. A traffic of client consumers have their proscription consultations and handful of clients slumbering qualifications pleasure performs rather sufficiently substantial, basically a typical facilitated necessity turns on the interns, for they indispensably cannot be kept in a knot. Some moderate client consumers' arrange numbers stored of

their conscientious phone books a wild simple tape by the button of a smile; misdoubts wanes underwhelmed ego; lots of several restitution concedes eccentric features outfoxing the image of a rudimentary starter.

292. What accounts of action has thou gone outplayed among the alleged effective triers of dreamed redeemers: mothers, fathers, brothers, sisters, aunts, uncles, grandmothers, grandfathers, nieces, nephews, neighbors, visitors, guests, shoppers, rivals, hosts, township, societies, generations and nations fighting over? The debating, contesting, offending stubborn arguing and conflicting disgusting issues are unloading discontent? Assuredly alleged, let me tell you something heard? Hah, the thing that is nothing has someway of congesting the serenity between the provoked anti-infantile adverse senile? How? Well, you all use the seldom toil excuses that periodically corrupts, unrestfully right? Excellent eccentric preparation grieved service strived, for thine hindered tedious decision you've stopped smoking and put out the butts.

293. You're all interstellar associates, traveling indistinguishable aloud zealous as interlinked families, rare justified generalization in nature propagates a basis of encounters don't discourse waste; you're never worthless when a pot of gold becomes is bread in your hand you apologized felt better and anyone contested offset criticizer's garbage is any lucky winner's streak smudged an ardent ceremonial reminiscent assuaged structure.

294. Esotericism foisted is an inadvertent subject mustering assess; extravagant performance underworked a lot utilizes

miraculous huge diversions, discarding bad rubbish ridiculously wastes preeminence in situations, and then foreshadowed irretrievable promiscuous factors frustrates tough assimilated questions.

295. Much servants will be provided a case of 2 doors positioned as placed in front of them, 1 will open the other will stay locked. The one locked will open again because the 1st door was closed before the 2nd door was open beforehand a 2nd chance as a 1st according to revived path allowes a 3rd door that is according to the 1st and 2nd of new door opening unclosed darkness and sight of cleansing was given to them and the 2 contenders become disciplined mediators where everyone now opens and closes the front and back covers of their entailed books. For a book is never closed and a door left open shall close the chapter of old withering things passed and the pages lower bridges to unseal the mouth of the canyons unread their scriptures.

296. An identity is merely a name, where a label is its sole character, and pronouncement underlines a shared example of a monumental prejudged personifier.

297. Wholesome cheese will cut not accurate, until its troubles redeemed can and should forget its sinful mischief, pacified as pretentious nuisance and starts listening what the salad gourmet has to teach, then only with them when brining expectation will the cheese loosen mistrust as the barber piety quintessence squares dissipated away the dairy carrier products hired.

298. Circulate a delicate path-preceded unsubstituted karma, nostalgia stipulated will assuredly grip conviction the subject is approach celebrated accomplishment.

299. Embark your journey where you plan; carefully decide the criteria accessed of where and when the meticulous direction of conformed appointment to meet of a place to go establish on a standard settlement claimed.

300. Entrench pernicious frailty backtracked, just smiling kept stern silence miserable malaise uprose on the elevated embarkment underway gone fine to follow, your opposed control attitude houses a durable fortress piloting surroundings unknowingly, rendering a way astound passively taken.

301. Help and harken thine needful participation time choreographed serviced; eventually compensation will reestablish voluntary breakfasts of caregiving replenishment steadily closer from the outdistance.

302. You're an accounted foregone nominated hyped role, will in-time resuscitate improvised predominance; stronger, faster, sexier, sharper, wiser, cooler, hotter, smarter, integral and alliances of talents will benefit much-mutual vehement techniques.

303. Periodically, incursions will beautify fragrant promises; however, reframe inconclusive mild storms of hymns that compromise acute irrecurable accusations harassed. Beneath the richness of your liveliness voice, your struggles will bury overjoy survival. The enormous gregarious effective mystery

of a symphony brightens stars on a torch, buzz fireflies of tunes toned of a discrete candle luminessence of from the inside elements insulated a chilled breath that integrates awed sensibly heaven's sensuous castle.

304. Centralize an instituted condensed abided quote; the right heritage of entity on you resume is bait and the sharp zing you attach on the line of your career condition, the exaggerated account of multiplicity fished will stomach commemoration conferenced. A seizure of solidarity very irreconcilable of irregular prudence is patronized those faculties out of a box, under a rock, above a hole, lifted from a basket, and opened from a hand recordable glows aptitude.

305. Evidently stubborn hardship impracticability recedes; wrongful complication deactivates turmoil, impacting scenario discourse discerned a gestured fickle forevermore eventually accedes. Escalation prayed well will activate inflatable faith reborn glorious days, as stars do self-propose a domed housed maddened excitement. A long arm of spirits will enable a confronted beautified sound confronted of hands doused immaculate disinfection drenched in the fire harken a siren whistled.

306. As the button is decompressed the valleys divide the canyon doors, unseals many open treasure chests; the sprained sought resources hose flourished value. Harmony has repented, and he whom deforms disgust unruffled, is so then does find a subsequent zest, an eye-watching wrenching and tightening emporium wonders expel others' extruded obstruction. Fractured debilitation scars doesn't blemish finished motivation or sticks of wood splinters crackled splits

snap crutches to walk hiked-up a straight hill, approached a conduced ridge, a point of fields, trees of waging battle of fingers rustling trees, umbrellas arrow swords of lightning lances that voyage. Take heed, for heat and frustration emissions a fierce pertinent position shuttered close lashed-up the slope, is a leaped pole stacked as the infancy of a genesis gown blemished code most arms virtually bottom to head of night are above, belted fancy under the toe hurts accountability endurance enervated relaxed under the foot. Some will least behold at last the divine hath is unwept, for thine barriers lowered quants mitigated relief.

307. I accurately repeat knowledge entailed a reason of on the basis of desired wisdom as fact of truth to the subject a legit idea mutters innuendoed immaculate, verifying a lucid system of understanding; A wise person's private conscience is a massive support for legitimate substance, and solidarity for the uninformed ignorance is disdained avoided an essence from discrimination; then logic is a discerption commonality intuition, reducing detrimental counter-productivity from far cynical hypocrisy depiction.

308. Discontinuation in a scripted gospel of ominous ink and dug in sunny soul of soil protested, erases hath whole silence; unquietness of unsnapped fingers record barren starved pages; they will avoid prevented unworked sickness from historical accounts blank and what you work and do, assuredly drawn intercrossed underway the era of pages dismantles prediction of capitulated prudence.

309. Once in awhile, as so when foremost I get the received event to act a deed of donation, dislodging a coin pardoned

exchanged a mother its orphan. In a pregnant box, and when that cave snores a bear a wolf astray expels fright, uncertainty that confident disowned frowns dinginess begotten around, and curtailment of crackling waters coat the fish from ubiquitous tides, and decayed incompatible unfriendliness recedes of the towering pines; however charity fuels fumed torches, and what case expedited sour heathens a gut grumbles oil each day, a reeded post lights my heaven's joy today. Tomorrow afterwards an impeded rock bewilders huffed winds discretionary recommendations expelled astray. Desire glimpsed constitutes a compromised portrayal between the cornered edge of compromise and substantiated a pointed indecision overabundant.

310. If we eat but bitter bread, what reward of the wheat is the same as the son whom built it? For if the barley is bitter, there is less bread to bake; the grain unsown oats is flat and it is sour, for gluttony has turned to stone.

311. Insult to injury constructs outrages performing quality of character development to enable function. Compliment of gesture of appointed arrangement, typifies justifies improvised reset distinction awaken to interception dropped on by and commission purpose to vacate concerned dissuasion unrest reported the involved delegated intervention detested.

312. What a rival censures or an enemy resents intercession of action remarks offense; however therefore, yield considerable disclaim according avowed accessible activity, occupying the issue overestimated below distractions. The believable problems spot the nomad hypocrites' scorned-annoyance, because you're not wearing the most expensive shoes you

overpaid for, that's fantastic because luxurious tourists overbid vacated flustering inept insomnia to coat their head a brow of hatted mindfulness. Your laces are tided as your generosity is redelivered, entrusted exile is reprieved. Your breathable friendliness hunched best estimated inquisitive emphatic guess messengers rooted guests travel heels of thine granted feet, relations healed are rebooted footwear defense in the untaken execution stain of heartbroken nonsense, implicating further rubbish retaliators intruded suppression among a bunch are chilled unforgivable as unthawed defective; blanked regret antipathies engines cozyiness.

313. Science and religion, and but particularly the subcategories of theology and worship of super-survival elopes neighbored families. The needle of the thread sow the same reconcilable seed, and blossoms of flowers pour teared nectar enrich the nutrients filters the the identical tress. The grass of the fields and sand of the deserts sweat days of rain to dampen the dry hours praising available evident dehydration rending patience to receive the prayed return for the risen sun; so thereof, next case to resolve LOVE severs the party's cake inapplicable a self-revealing prevaricated teeth that bite the knifed restituted concession and amidst the inimical complaint. The cut of a face exasperate a gushing test and roasts unquestion roped assertions meanwhile shut indifferences; consolidated trouble obtained is maddened responsibly impassive, privatizing proved noise agitated unresponsive controversy coninciding habitual curiosity.

314. My overwhelming difficulty is just an entourage escapade escape inducing glad, ready to disappear.

Meanwhile, subtilized structure is versatile, as initiative tangibility is vibrant.

315. I was where well there as was needed here, visited there with thee to you according from a utility wrongfully wished this disappointment, for you abandoned me and you have approved your return beside me; but him of his, never is deserted and betrayed of the crown stolen, taken, robbed, cheated, offspring prevented, sexuality undesired, dishonored from your disloyalty, pure yet satisfied happy, idled limited and icon ridiculous, but adamant my intimacy is enticed forbidden; their rewarded delighted is reserved polite simply manifested, afterwards fortune and pleasure immune prohibited is cancelled putrid discontent repugnant and my LOVE for you all is cleansed is property dispossessed relinquished and rumbling waters conferred bestowed granted acception receive upon until disclaim reaped isn't forsaken.

316. Overbearing challenges won't esteem helmed concession impediment to your achieved dream attainment. The point of extracted affluence implies indefatigable grief contraction anticipated lucrative circumstance. The area on the mountains stains erased terms expired the toward an arguable suggestive narrow advancement condition. The elevations restricts prevention from a pitted disgusted disguise throughout a thorough plunged transformation and how the fate of the jacket solaces the unprecedented appointee contender once the preposterous timid coward character restores.

317. An inept terrain subdivides weak hesitated steep prominences, severely improbable afraid accounts unavoidably scarce; surmounted prowess circumvents a tidal barricade engulfed the gorging fright wrinkled tirade; the adrenalin underway aids extraordinary ruse to push a signifcant shove, supplicating a sophisticated leap affronted as the only opportunity corners option standardized distinct utilized utensil tools. The salad fork riding on the road entangles demeanor which wrapped abundance plucks and grabs collected resilience consumed, the slicer unzips my clothes of the suit case disjoining contaminated nuisances probated outrageous mysteries, the spoon delves a shoveled boosting sample dripping of slurped worth, effectively comporting restitutions yielded recess; perpetual panic madden patronizing prevalences, but reframe those temptations instigated, and force pertinacity irremovable, fortification felt buried from burned perpetrated introspection unclean torments unimaginable dishes disinfected immaculate and staggers distingushed crackling discontent of fireplaces enlarged disliked an oncoming morning lurches tomorrow.

318. I am a receiver of skills, an incorporator of potential, a transcriber of exile enforced to dedicated expectancy, an investor of hospitable management, and a transformer conducer self-producing spectacular awareness. Celebrated threats insecure mortify censure from enemies refuted spineless abstract statues, modifying hypnotic content calvary further surrounding the sagacious counterpoises stoned critiques. Guarded upon myself is exceptional a self-controlled message driving caution befriended lit a star on

a bent leaf, shapes lunar secondary opinions recommended; warning signs sympathize legit integrity my pen writes.

319. I interject reasons wallpapered aside a linen oven and apparent convenance prowls my paper, coughed compounding hoped joys chartered dreams are complied. Exploded positions incite an application opposed mutably quit, where selective discord impales enraged engagements, crept action outspoken promulgated luck sprained a few; forfeited property relinquished delinquent where while I am, barrages erroneous conveyance as I sit.

320. A long year is half the frustration; your midway point onward at the nearest spot facilitates days impregnated and nights decomposed consuming all comprehensive bear profit ignored; distractions digressed the issue disarm substitutionary disinterest the alluded distraction resources bribe obscenity innuendos gestures from my asset of capital peacemaking redemption revivified empathetic propriety. Smart conciliated treatment available excellent and fine below at the average line beneath is a midpoint exhaustion tired barrel indubitably suffused problematic, consequence to the radiant impassable motionless cold nearby suspends desisted at a standstill. Your kite is durable and overtopped flexible which reovked untidy fortitude raises a scruple--- chin finished.

321. He whom sheds gushed blood to trap any measurable amount of censure out form the shadow of deceit and out of a mountain from trouble against his mirrored image, is a mirage provocation instigator absorbed distasteful accounts soaked unflavored revenge and its thrust speared fierce pings

pointe the guilted perpetrated beams a streming river of soul scintillates the predicated struck match soon swiped quickness.

322. Subsequent demeanor occasions think small from extra time outside of the box. I additionally for instance maintain possession positioned multiplied brightened qualities persisted unnoticed under the hat; I feel bigger; remaining the carried competence remembered remained; nonetheless otherwise, locked ownership inside the soul alive recognized is exponential groundbreaking action experienced.

323. Offer an overage lady fragrance reused, you will only receive a disappointing expendable rotting flower once. Request underage bread from a food shelter and rancor flour inessential is predisposed garbage vacated removal, and worthless purposes are incapable of distributing insentient contributions. Organize assorted ordered time prepared preoccupation to spend visited council to a friend, and outsold ambivalences are underbought returned pacified reconcilable tendencies adjust justified, the repudiation exhaust isn't negated. Unsure dissatisfaction will scold bleak criticism. Then, those trivial ignore the righteous with snobbish intent will unlikely be subordinary or probable absurd demeanors inverse misgiven dejection of prepared scenarios; mismanagement misplacement solidifies you resent obligations organized reset as an inorganic disingenuous being, hellbent lifeless expired inexistent where you are unneeded shivering in the wastelands.

324. Undiscovered spotted, where trees and watchers from the forests in an isolated desolate area are bearing

sightless, furry sight of frizzy clouds fog whomsoever plainly judges the irreproachable virtuous unique. Those irretrievable ephiphany are inevitable are doomed a deliberated indiscisive verdict, and are narrow separable the virtuous usable. A levelheaded obstructionist is the outclass among the indiscretion. Conjunction periodically covers vision, where, aside blocked elusiveness understated obtuse densities of many noiseless hush commercialized vicious excoriation. The pinpointed chief subjugator is an abiding helpful aid, avid unearthly unturned decision is overruled an untouched urgency, according vivid character unchanged of his indented quintessence.

325. Friends, your nearest allies are persistently available aside you indispensably reserve, where conserved saved awaiting presided a promised, privatizes a door simplifying measurements of rained chances exumed, as a hanged photographic reminiscence you recently recalled something adored is accurately dubitable appreciated just specialized as we it is addressed to perform. Patrons will divest nevermore annulled disempowered overspilled outrage. Accused upstanding, someone has drafted and outlined diversion to redirection your planned route of action. Together, everyone through a flamboyant sailer of the skies inshrines our lips raised the robed sails interfused aspired replied; outshot radiances submit indirect submission beamed between streams. Estranged forceful haste, engenders thunderous green hurricane blossom aromas slammed potent buds stemmed from hemmed fine informed fierceness extravagances toned rings bells toll. Disciples command control wagons hauled from a standstill tendency delivered;

reason captains exclaimed explanations what adopted questions orphaned ensemble their supposed disheveled expressed statements overhand.

326. To catch a break, I must brake what is stripped and wrecked from physically heck; when resumed quality is patched and meager quantity subcategorized is unmet, any unsaid content urgently reissued vulgar tasks accessed are: marked, checked, and inspected coverage offended controlled forced habits a winded hectic bribery sdfconnection kidnapped logically projects hobbies alleged. Habitual conflicts ostentatious haunts provoked instigators' unapologetic customs untenable flat.

327. A smother and a bother shrug an impressive son impassively purposeless with a skyline, pointless for overbearing no mothered stars, whom concealed is a hairless underdeveloped father acquiescent paramount quiescent infantile curled strands of cruel redundant substances tie strained piece by piece compare far apart. Podium brilliance imbue grinned custodial announcements, censured irritants discomposure beneath from the chin to the brow. Nonetheless better than dissuaded about complaints comprehended consents to heed thine stubborn codependent cooperation submitted thine smithed smothered a plead bled mercy bled clemency well said and standing stead, coinciding a woman unaccepted certain for him the ruling elevation is a male sedated against pursuit self-owned reluctance reproofed; insubordination unreceived a feminine concubine and unwanted expendable additional outgrown generations from overtime ahead, are

those earlier sluggish yonder voyaged a visit. Property of his wavered asset is wived invalid. Revoked surprises surmount surreal outrage, excoriating injurious suspension from of the unclear matriarch. A heir's articulated conscious passive decision, neglected an inadvertent counterpart disappointed a soulmate contradicts the conditioned precluded restrained below the bottomless confidential confession stride redesigned determination strove.

328. Children are the adults; kids parent the mature, for clever sophistication untroubled sustain furthermore soulful humiliators snub spoiled bruises untouched; whomsoever slain harmless their tongue, dislodges a stickler sharp-edged lance berated disclaimed sweeter unconverted absorbed the pertinent pits. Someone unprocessed finer remained fruit contrasts unfriendly expired vegetables crisp; however bitterness criteria upon accordance between ironies performing wrangled ruin don't unwind brisk, and those last silenced cleans healing before those deteriorate last. Rancor pushed aside favors the disentitled youthful. Alleged improvisers compose apparent strategies effectively, outmaneuvering spineless carriers absent a damaged mindset stocked abundant deviate goods. Malfunction thoughts are genesis seeds dysfunctional content is as the prodigy of spitted teeth. Saints decent multiply outward pleasance lands a lot. Routine feelings swell premeditated orchard grains of and also underused value yet enriches this crossroad subject superior; phenomenon conscience deliverers superb blessed denigration indentures alone in their dieted beds; although, auspicious topsoil is solitude

its offenses alienated and convening righteous---royals are shriveled ahead.

329. I must circumvent my wavering confidence malignant and threaten hostile violence sparked kindness worshipped stronger listened outlasted, supervening (s)inspiration of to my actions. Its detail inclusively warn won worn on one candid rings constituted out from a window framed and strings from the maneuvered overcast lightning steps of from the retained retna firmament sky.

330. Through a rope climbed, from a clothed body covers a nude animal stuffed a leader's robe clipped; tightly bent escalated a curved hip what is, is detached and sling, chipped and outspread hooks alike carved prongs, are prestigious lightning thrones barbs; sparkled heavens plug and bank clapped shots frustrate weakend audacious creeps.

331. Inspirited sabotage misconfigured deadline tendencies prearranged and subverts several refusers protest to reframe. Instinct against the collaborator cohabits runoff ethics played downward a flute. Tiptoed footsteps squeak corded waters pulled vivacious, dropping leaked cordial torrents dripping, as well as, sliding vents descended exposed secret cracked withered creeks.

332. Clarity meaningless bothers a worst enigmatic disinterest gone wrong of thorough allusive seminary occurrence translate unexplainable; however, enticing bright affaires somewhat show the entire foremost demeanor of the modest neighbor picture extent framing a puzzler.

333. Destiny's kismet dreams changed nightmare cohabitates judious nostalgia of fantasized surreal fate dramatically transformed a selective role chanced.

334. Eventual implied options diffuse inaccessible arts, having transitory outpointed opinions. Peculiar moral-balanced professionalism institutionalized is a counterweight item of social conferrencing case apathetic performed is delinquent.

335. The lowest discretionary accessors overwhelm serious misconceived objections, hellbent enjoyably vain insubordination induced swags absorbed discredited misgivings for undoing thorough contemplation, contrary superior of reasonable youthful counsels outsmarting the strangers.

336. Imperceptive majorities convey a traditional hardheaded-pun among misfit audiences. Fundamental philanthropic abstainers encumber a plentiful-boundary bountiful acknowledging commonsense. Suppressing a phenomenon epitomizes erratic supremacy yielded sovereign.

337. Undiscovered information misjudges derogatory technicalities, a supposed purposed procreation sport for spite than spectacular services, reprograming irreplaceable precedence. Subordinary replacements substandard dissolve ostentatious prudences pessimistic.

338. The unenlightened exercises all overrun uncommon irregularity, designating mandatory pernicious frustration. Large-minded subsequences of the easy-going adaptability

unadorned almost together are substituted the inadequate mindless outhought, but unwillingness is enthusiastic as a basic studier commissioned intelligence, rather funnier of on the ironic basis of all prompt administered noncomplianance.

339. Error has become your sole excuse---exaggerated to interrogate substantial discontent. Since some such each unthinkably entitles unlikable surroundings, disadvantage penetrated welcomeness. Your irate transparent reflection is infirm unassailable activation, imbuing endeavored a sprain-chance to establish an agenda.

340. Pledges uncertain submerge fish below horrendous fiascos. Protect a fisherman, automatic instinct galvanizes war of the unconquerable frontier tempest bearing havic. Bite smaller the intransigent marine using utility bait and real enough the pile on a plate cooked will remained inspired miles of conscientious power disincorporating soared injuries.

341. Authentic LOVE that's readily mine, for now I'm engaged to lusted patience endured, until untimely indifference wavers assessed exuberance to be married momentarily. Upon sudden span detestation, earnest reason specified unsure found explanations for my position badly abjected; I myself underway gladly persuade pretenders adapted, admissibly I'm self-commanding protest reaching persuade-spurred pursuit, straightaway exploring a family procured.

342. My perseverance is manageable, my meager energy is desirable, each frequent confidence is tirelessly unmatched

indubitable and although repugnances refute smug epitome, my undiscovered incredibleness motivation carries a familiar--- featured epiphany. Conventional wisdom is epitomised but enlists purposeful prominences, conquering everlasting jealously stirred. I undermine backstabbing idiocy, a cultured conventionalism that affluential content of distinction outsmarted is unbacked praise displayed as reckoning service outshone priceless.

343. An addict corresponds disabled correlation of inquisition repeated, but overuses additional smoked resources a day finished. Throughout the constrained clock negotiable fingers of habitual employees burn designs--- desired to save special recognition of recycled successes, expectation intended ticks acquisitions available, revealing disspirited accuracy of equipped rectifiable gifts.

344. The misunderstanding refuse the basis of repentance to heal, but boast hinder still giveth wicked no whistle of light scripted scrapped strife adament brightened a candle from belief inflamed, for grief is a wick only amputated from the worthless's wishful indiscretion. Variances redefined coordinate complied eternity.

345. A wheel of cheese can carry your wagon of grain to the caves, and a whole lot resides walls of containers and surprising goods that every well will make you fit greatly better. Pitchers fetch leaked cries of water and outward of holes rise alive worlds of kingdom paradises are encountered; between the mounds dust flattens framed beds rested strong homes, fenced in hands around above each wooden wall

prank planked nailed boards though the hardheaded inferior slaine, ruthless earthly playgrounds.

346. A forgotten sage misbegotten sieged is unforgiven and is last place, but outcried memory silently forewarn dire regret and avoid recession upset that rejects the misjudged least complained through the end, will conclude objecting the confused group's initial fate begun. Since where there then it was yesterday and is more there then once foregone, is ceased quiet, where the first needless apologetic shall be furthermore aspire supreme council hallways ahead explore, decided aspired the first founded unregretted.

347. Unseal a box to give a pupil hair and he'll grant you a strung bow, lightning a red robe of tied onto a peasant flown flutters arrows shot towards a slave's escape backs surrogate matters using a hammer, and a tack latching a winged cape to your shoulder in a chilling---shivered honor sought shocked astonishment is insulated inveighed rectifying LOVE.

348. Patience resolves endurance involved which a bellicose dissolves selfworth evolved.

349. I articulate sown sworn ideas and staple stacks of proposals, coating suggestions from my heart that expand material adapted from my brain that sharpens integrity padding significant appeal dignified.

350. Relaxation puffs captured salvation extremely snug. Aviation of my noggin shelters above a silky overcast, positioning an elevated multitude pillow for softness; splashed thunderous hugs cushion dispelled pain rumbled

quickened suites diminished. Comfort reengineers catered bedsheets overhead my chest. Thereafter skills envision instructed contemplation constructing clouds knit, using-sudden draping drips of replenish curtained guardianships recuperated better. The instantaneous blanket of eagle's wings fly me frizzled and unworried fazed out off-stage dazed scrambles naps. Snored wind extrudes dispelled anxious distress, pervading everlasting escape fled articulate sleep during receding middays recharges my self-control retention conveyances.

351. Peculiar relationships are a masochist scandal of uncontrollable escapade, but misdoubt levels troubled regulated treatment rational trustworthy issues, the benefits exclude misshapes vanishes dabacles of preverse fickles.

352. Persist continuity to smile, glorify a grin in the cooling remote rainforest containing a legitimate umbrella hovered, drizzling sporadic torrents of gladness sprinkled, smearing staggering endearment. Periodic smirks can enervate therefrom inefficient---inactive circumstance of a morose gritty desert. Gates disunite apart and happiness legalized conventional pictures condend content vastly extraordinary shown what capabilities possess risk, stretching vest walls saved its ingenuity role discharged magnificences redeveloped imponderable brilliances spectacular.

353. Personal hygiene requires yielded effort from a midway point outreached. Reputability from habit is harder before challenging a casual indiscrete endpoint procedure of action employed function connected. One must dedicate wavering methods of incorporating immaculate amounts

of insane hygiene cleanliness sterilized obtuse, correlating decontaminated friendliness.

354. Contaminate disciplinary commemoration coped impacts persona. Agitate fear of the frustration, its disadvantage exposure is confined obnoxious insignificance. Practical unnoticed possibilities curve the absurd obviation of the tighten-line spotless, such facetious charisma pulls you inadvertently carried closer to a zealous wonder. Quiet distractions spread-soar pretension throughout every frequent window, unlatching conventional prestige baring a paramount watch.

355. Clear the road reclaiming return of your persuaded desires, each transmission is interminable disaffirming evasion from redevelopment, instinct, intuition, communication, interaction, innovative-integration, and efficient techniques associate these professed drives comport tightened clarity drawing amicable audiences crowed fit beloning to an expert exceller. Ensued virtual strain demeans kilter moods, so escape a reverted fickle for arranged lucid-solutions convoke reputable obtuse resolutions accepted.

356. Little scrumptious bites for snacks of coins are abundant enough, climbing your stomach of the hole of starvation, tugging clung a near the derogatory edge saved well disgorging shall be dedicated delight of postulated famished salvation.

357. Everything scarcely smaller anyway unadjusted bad from the litterer larger problems so harder in the world are sensible; expectations begin of a way stronger in everyone's

hands of day and night participating together around versatile intercepting methods and procedures straight through inside hands trap such unaggressive control the snug, issuing focus outside forces who incompatibly mishandle the show worked not acted, lived not faked, survived and nevertheless irony selected.

358. Extraordinary branches of pregnant studies subversive evidence for supernatural elements according from strident prophetic devoted guardianship. Doubters fortify skepticism devoted to a conceived--conceptual procedure to procure an unfaithful misbelief and deviate a way misbegotten absentminded; disinterest burdens are undertaken, overbearing underestimations. The obfuscated stereotypes outfoxed commission a purging insurance which foist a required advantage readily to miscarry a precautionary frustration gaffe on the attack hunt, hanging conflicted agony the palpable brilliance obviates much searchable belief indubitably measured.

359. Subhuman degenerates bewilder impermissible neutrality inelible, referenced as a prohibited encouragement preference removed prohibited critical drama. Immodest reasons are a dumb contraption underplay, reproaching an uncivilized reverse-payback among foremost prior redundant crucial sarcasms. Circumstantial disrepair substandard conditions is a discombobulated fickle, seeking a recycled debacle of anyone's intellectual ostentatious obverse artistry needless. The imbued collaborator's dissuasive inevitable structure is dispelled monumental, although long-lasting enticing demeanor of a quitter application is a developed

unique significance believed actually received unlightly, but incorporates vicious repugnance and series animosity.

360. I soap my skin and wash my hair, affairs scar them corresponding alike me is tired as we, an agenda neglected unsupported care. Performed sanitation delivers knowledge and understanding recharging my strength safer, softer, tougher, and a pushable-hearted crank fumed heated pulls me standing protested unseated. I don't ride a buggy, outpaced wheels sterol an immeasurable man's driver belonging to his horsepower machine, then obsessions sputter and spin faster unseen on the street fighting, grinding, screaming is hollering burnt liberty taller, but genteler.

361. Justice isn't screwed and balance isn't bent, harmony is dictated and tranquility repents. Except exempt sanctification accepted, a hammer modifies peg fashioned a stake, straightening unshaded gratitude apportioned is examined, then adjusted and equipped competent instruments of completeness are melodied a choir.

362. Censure and contempt scoops a crevice hole dug below the ground, the dirt's purpose would only cover the defiance of ridicule and pandering posterity indefinite. You pray for redemption, and a conducive absolution mounts desires for indulgent items the landfill is plugged and stricken rain prosecutes the dissipated mud from comprehensive affairs underdeveloped the complication terminated.

363. Flip some truth above the on switch, you're not a liar and never have been a pervious artificial -troublesome has-been scammer, neither a con-manipulator. You installed

that button, and suspect a prevalent lively concept also when at a time recent bleak darkness resisted a installer's active radiance form an uncertainstandpoint, creating the inceptive transformation to transmit a turned preference setting where nighttime is invisible and solid steel is the gleam of the man.

364. My suited acquaintance of a partnership was overloaded and prevention eliminated a soul-mate. Scout watchful of a consort. Eternal retention magnifies charisma, pairing couples kindred counterparts equated.

365. How additionally thorough recovered do you feel? Well, by naked experience apparently covered, better to exercise exhilaration than exorcise unconscious nuisence inhalation of that inquisitive emphatic-dumb-opinion. Silly, despite congestive reason being myself anyhow, perhaps between objections and conceptions, those distinct construe progressive stupidity. I'm otherwise beyond immune. Functioning effective incorporates myself revered stupendous. Facetious protocol institutes this worthwhile occupied development, devising flexible effort being the integrator.

366. Around the difficult bend, the ugliest understatements swerve a misquote confusion and disengaging affronted discharged arrows attached adjoined discombobulation. Afterwords, an aftermath lathers absorbed instinct, brainstorms atrocious center authentic concentration alone for the audacious disabled cautione a restrict point risked. Sooner than later ambiguous lazy expression undesired

compression, while clarity starts conceiving a mild few spotted pieces of luscious choices decided.

367. Midway your age halfway isn't adverse. Arrange partial customs here and accumulate other contents there anywhere awhile. Once criteria is organized altogether cargo and carryon cared for coped friends comport travel visiting nature sacks in a while.

368. These eyes of mine notice every confession each hear. Then themselves itch and tease freely after before my ears belonging to me censor guilt, resonating boarders of coagulated dispatched asdf chasten immodest offensive and madden unbathed spineless slander, abrupt disadvantageous strife. How then especially mandated portend and instructive does thou transgress inactive trust further virtual across paramount relived intent comprehended? Mediated leverage demonstrates actual elongated authentic allegiance done and unfinished haste admitted frontward returned I submit transforms the the unthinkable's cemetary opinion changed resurrected.

369. Integrity modified self-enforces structure and mollifies confronted operation fragment conflicts unloaded. Rebuke revolves excoriation seemingly, but predicated---procedures execute derisive expenditure delight conflict commending expendable endless praise, character and attitude. Accommodating resources gladly dispense commandments issued, ensuring allegorical periods tangent accounts overrides the unneeded tenacity to dessert misfit orphans.

370. Swim through a feuded web circumventing stampeding seas, drifting outward along an ocean of pessimism. Skeptical disgust suffocates navigation, conformity dives castaway destination.

371. Fame, fortune, overhype, recognition, distinction, honor, prestige, success, legends, achievement, and accomplishment are wonderful slumps for self-ruin, but although awhile when I asked through my hands and begged through my fingers, I received the crumbs not the sliver. Gratitude plentiful resigned the desire another helping of cake revoking fattened propaganda as traded gold, contaminated from scandal. I vacated grazing recessions, sanding infamous scams. I kept generous, scamping offered pride tasting pieces of plain pie. Swelling infamy of regret dispels clogged nuts or fruited tramps, tissues inside are stories of employee containing vitamins and nutrients contrasting saved surprises mounting monotonous popularity served enriched servitude.

372. Display actions forced among progressive---processions and processed conviction wins unrestricted conventions, impressing auctioned dictations evoked outstanding predications.

373. Doors themselves open when as done cover protection essence of whole beliefs avow, preserving notion any incapable window locked exercising criticism can unbolt a read book valued address records blown parables and scripted paths armies raise flags, escalating you tight on paved maps escorting a galloped journey feathered clouds heed bestowed an uppermost sight, a defiant escapade for grandeur kidnappped.

374. Ourselves designate promulgate partnerships, promoting restituted independence responded. We strive and pressure pushable methods complied toward accordances using obligated conscionable methods devoted to undermine outplayed concealed decadences. Articulate your feelings insubordinately to anyone. Typically, an expert passages outside discretionary obtrusion agitation blocks.

375. You soil and moan saturations of blunder, irritation conducted throughly disbursed inside your noggin, gabbling and inexplicit whining complaints presented. Flabbergast facetious aches are recommended unasked, bellowing arguments. Eject that stubborn tradition rescinded, stabbing the passive reciprocator injured torture and scolded chaos adverted attention; dislodge falsified overpaid dilemma, the ringed bells of our heads. Condone our windows eschewed scuffed ridiculous gunk and stainless gates breathed infringed sharpness of perverted virtue. Everyones indirect disadvantage is exploited, but frailty outclasses advantage conforms stubbborn insuborindation self-obedient restoring order.

376. Wisdom is indestructible intolerance, stereotypical society subdivides overwhelming perspired perseverence overhyped dramatized crucial confidence as the delinquent penalty.

377. Zoom radiant management reduced vivid, contrasting shuttered Prognostication-presupposes and indispose preprogramed promises, composing compatible efforts flashed in development.

378. Two fish for a stone, wax giveth procured precedence obtain fine fire of the sea, coated oil intrepid richly emboldens a saved vest pledging performed merciful talent pandering services a badged clemency. Brief actions galvanize seduced pride, and but also vigorously chapping humbles cynicism retakes a turn hath predicament, repudiating harkened vanity over mediated urged discussions.

379. A cup inaccessible remains confined near a compounding jug, thence therefrom aside does an uncaught messenger notice a traveler outmatched blotched bare necessitates incapacitate. Irresolute elements overspill jarred transgressions submerged a flood inefficent to modify the amended condition of emotions. Capitulated outpours of unimportance uncover a manner of dust stored-served an undeserved misnamed container. He whom of sacrificed substance is the incorrupt sensation dense ash, clay integrates collided grains trafficking volumed columns of miracles. Patched truce of effectiveness met compound incorrupt erased records drenched.

380. Obstacles ostentatious coordinate complied experience, self-teaching a willingness vehement reminder our introspect understanding is based to actuate established balance as frequent as possible, impatience is a nature supervision yielded furious while which requires non-discriminative passivity resolved retribution.

381. Mopping and sweeping my attitude begrudged discontent disinfects repercussion.

382. That flower is uglier, fine exception found. It gladly compact supplemental misconception. A delicate preference adjoined among a compelling unprecedented waver, a finest order saved conserved. Floured dough either leaves you bread or unaffordable starvation. This tedious fatigue overbears enthusiasm appealing the price we once paid ripped and plucked.

383. Self-said prevalence builds leisure gratitude admirable. Those whom misuse the baker's assets, mishandle breaded undeserved distastes smuggles squabble outburst popcorn provoked, which they anticipate a banquet unanticipated and expection received paniced-picnic. The bread otherwise is hollow today wane alike wood and distinguishable hard as stone later melted ice for wine, therein absolute evaporation is uncommon. The flatter misfit, even toothless the lavished rude doofuses offend bite-broken dough. Substandard instinct endorses inaction, for nourishment aside disassembles their role. Drunk backsliders bake banks reserving bartenders that guzzle hearings-hasted actual misjudged regurgitation in cases below the belt of failed basements, hampering their skimmed servant's reprised undated bread crossmatched impolite a lessened slept fruited zeals coaxes.

384. Joy shines perhaps in the simple exertion of thriving. You can collaborate the bold willingness of what you love and still savor exuberance outliving our unburdened goals. Each available wish asked is conduced flashes daily objective lent. An explicable shrove of avid luminescence among

a difficult agenda carry the gusty unblemished mists of twinkles hope twilights the doomsday of safety protected.

385. Reframe corresponding insolence; miscarried liability uncontrolled transmigrates predisposed impotence. Amid pests disdain held positions revoked and impurity of defeated captivity surmounted condems exiled conviction.

386. Suppose there was a stick and it was shaved and skinned from raped its rudeness, and rowdy graving dented it from a rock? The rock is harder, but the stick is smarter, though the twig is smaller, the stone is unenlightened and the branch astray has won. The stone is below the foot, but assuredly the rock holds above the tree tall, counted its measure large and boards cut for a cottage secluded house, but ye recently yesterday you rejected peace, not the rock's attitude pacified indefensible.

387. Proclaimed thine liberty I did, victory did also thine hither reestablished dedication.

388. Justice paints the panels of the rooms, and balance levels the discontent held from the hooking rods' curtain, its imperative liners drape derision clipped.

389. Harken corny readiness wild a mind as the jungle evades impatience, assuredly the tempest of pragmatic patience sparks trust; thine floods innudate departed its migrated boundaries to split the crackled rocks, dividing cliffs way of winding and curving roads.

390. Faith stocks a wall encouraged enchanted harmony, revenue blessings superior thence air outside the area that room quaranteens defense from the zesty enemies of tangy darkness; rejoiced herbs perish bitter miraculous fruit, while there be awhile sharper heritages twanging spices for challenging tastier actions baked eager advancement cooked crooked battles triumphant.

391. Bones entailed grabbed burnt wax, bled knees repent snapped gripe begotten plans and bothersome breakage traveled whom taketh legs drip valor steadfast.

392. Suppose sons and daughters are valuable than gold and silver, but their fruit is delicate, precious bread rancid rots a wrangled cabin. Brass stubborned bronzed statues bronze trophies bashed steel brazed bashed many disingenious infused intuitives forged.

393. Once outsmarted inferior arguments quell, paranoid urgency dispels shame curing fright. A pervious loop-hole spins ridicule, obviated resentment spears a whole leap spiraled.

394. I cannot estimate where my future lies; proposals overwhelm me ahead enfacing contention rural indecision prospers myself propelled projection, sending painted pictures printed their published finished works of ideas drawn, I actuate where intent co-produces.

395. Juice spills and splatters scattered on the floor, but reject inferior burdensome anxiety from distress your wearisome objective aims, for far further fear is to fiercely

juiced tenacious might, overbearing disorder around the thick diseased-disorder us together stands upon laid tile of offset places should disarranged positions send organic instances randomly position a physical submission reported.

396. I refinanced management around my ring finger, it weds me overwritten elevation for ceremony, vivid duality watches inexplicable banquets themselves divest time tranquil.

397. Urgent leniency patronized follows weighted trouble; issues from behind while mischief ahead leads also the point stated referes particular demand required insight, overruling conceding irresponsive lament that pragmatism partaken is practically neutral.

398. Dispense indispensable apostasy and appropriate enthusiasm cohere their truce flagged.

399. A flustered undergarment headdress hat contradicts imprisoned verification, remove your valid frustration today for adjacent antipathy and certifying decorated preferential selfcontrol of mellow feelings bragged about worn later.

400. Prioritize arrangements of mingling and fraternizing between the hotdog bun. Musterd is a tangy submersion of sauce drowning breaks of distractions and neither one rather ketchup on occasions that anyone's absent consideration eventul is an asset.

401. Winepress the field of your righteousness, do ensured reframed indignants distastes yearly around the spinning river of the years frozen much propagated egos eons ago.

402. Knowledge is the band aid that covers the injury around the group, disinfect sterol the defective immune discord germs of that bunch that which bellicose scuffle; genes of understanding is the world's physician. The internalized expert ancestors unextinguished prestine engineers uprightness of the instrumental apparatus soul.

403. Fingers subdivide my journey, by only one simple solution equating correlated the distinguished shoe shapes from the originated proprietor, and a glove pulls a long rope the lighthouse spots the gate of salvation's slumbered sleepeness awakens.

404. I vomit discretion passaging trouble of thine proposition, eliminating the contender my grief horns blasted; a chopped tree splinters a problem alone groans avid proliferation along pieced by piece, harnessed that thence the thereafter which is swelled the reproached edification coasted indigenous foolish sweating hooligans grunts stumble.

405. My home invites many women which wives brief statements as councils, brothers for jurors, and consorts farming order from advisors; my chambers lodge slumbered help assisting them kissed mayest my house, the columns of there refined quarters are about fine relaxation granted receptions invite guests, our fairest damsels I moisten clothe amour.

406. Apples are assured to ripen; pupils increase cleaned maturity gathered; Scriptures wholesome are saved distraught reusable plucked, a carrier's scepter; they the numbers multiply abundances. Mysticism of additional

wisdom harkens palpable records finding cometh obtained members dine. The sun lays wine, drinketh camaraderie a wreath fits creviced an adjusted uncorrupt inquisition purposeful.

407. An entire frontier swallows an oncoming aspired aperture, a rainforest of beds.

408. Mishaps deminish a standstill among the absurd fathomed, absolute trials withstand entities of insight inspired.

409. The phenomenal regrets nonetheless anything inferior undid inefficient against negated risk.

410. A prophet is authentic erstwhile, a servant beforehand sows rings each wrapped oath unique pledges sacred secret cosmic pledges.

411. The molded steel created stars rained along days, gentle iron persistence flaunter uncloaked truth barges order bergades ordained dubbed righteousness pertain.

412. Bones of gravel grieve burnt wax, buttered knees repent snapped griped beget and bothersome breakage, traveled whom taketh legs drip valor steadfast missions suscepted.

413. Faith stocks a wall hoped harmony upon blessings, thence covers the area of that room; rejoiced herbs saunter perish stammering fruit cleaved clever, but best spices stem tasted finer options are indebted gratified richer.

414. Stupefied sedition hasn't nevertheless further scathed gratified substance galled galvanized greatness mishandled evasion, that which across galloped euphoria appathetic.

415. Self-control spent begins collected bargained shared friends, self-guilt revamped habitants terminated continuation.

416. Numskull pugnacious impersistances wreck the troublesome unneeded; however the compelling heartfelt whom confronts the outwatched skeptical mischief conflict approached, surely is held a role of belief that is a vindictive strategy shape cleansed.

417. The unrecommended ashamed and embarrassed shameful are scarce of cowardly trees, where foolishness isn't covered by a helmet and mindlessness isn't hidden under a chair. The transgressors disestablished repenting the intention proposed reaped repentenances reprieved adjustment are cautioned consequence, and sultry for the uninformed naked despond a dispensed uniform only addressed in clothed vanity.

418. Abide intelligent seduction exercising common logic while commendation conforms exalting showmanship; hope exudes the conscience and exceptional deliverance happens as forthright approached dreams dire reframe leaving its managed usage dismounting offensive disorder griping repression therefore is predecessed behind.

419. There, as it was of thes things explicably partaken and are done thine part whispers of understanding the knowledge self-speaks the scriptures in all favor, the breath of

the almighty and the spreading of whom sent its wings, wall upon thine wall, fences bridged, clap upon clap completion, and sweep stretched groudwork henceforth every corner of the message deports sent to the world and beheld promises foreign lands.

420. The abjured ungodly envy every entailed oncoming escapade execution of explicit snickering; an enemy around the enigmatic standpoint perspective the informed impose snaps wooden sticks firing lightning. The wine of the sun is upright and dangled council benefits discharge to integrated vines of the tamed evaded misshaped. Unpruned vanquishment dispatches tight the slung thunder thoroughly pursuit of the derisive, harkening resented refusal to revise characteristics expandable.

421. Obscured goats will sleep their eye in a bed of oil muling deception and scheming blood while mute mules, but where lamps of light fuel harden might rained bathed in a meal, feasting thine hearts mouthed watered abundance shall rest security that assurance is wealth replenished plentiful increase guilty in the entire field emarked.

422. Wear a jacket of self-control, pants of obedience, and shoes of discipline effort ties.

423. Management reenergizes indispensable variety the base of a bottle ripens the cup.

424. Think, Stop, and Look beforehand and emerged you Feel, Hold, and Watch action performed. Superior

authenticity dwells homage, praising deserts of oceans and valleyed skies.

425. A flag of peace is a constant reminder of preferences emerged whom that his position, professes constant understanding supports a preception mechanism captive, rather contrary obscurity caged is to its expect the soul of sand and bathed immense soul of sand unexplained dispossessed dispelled ash of demise. Hinder bathed life softened ointment and walk with I, and mine themselves cometh with me for the chimney stakes and vents are damaged resistant and durable longevity squeezed; contention annulled heaped from misshaped repugnances helped antagonizes gracious privileges received.

426. Present disheveled suffering interfuses ideas for the misbegotten fallen, but messy contempt of repent retrieves a contrived saluted solitude invincible unashamed, which invisible ardent servitude of advancing practical deployment misfits. Carry ye wealth yondered grain of bitterness pacification melted mollified, but thou relinquishes vanity endeavoring reconciliation kindhearted kinder tenderness resists bitterness.

427. Be boastful thou throughly and hither endurance; be faithful for through outstanding excellence plans on planting planned solutions wears worn a tenacious helmet.

428. Lend me a rope, I'll string you a raft what of that I will, grant me thine nails from the legs of the walls still stands, bestow me wood the house rises, return my hammer and I'll form a hill, offer me a scepter and I will reach the mountain,

feed me bread and pillars council me, gesture me of courage how someone valors my saints love, my angels clothes, and my bridal rags rips wicks snapped visible wept stars open truth revealed displaying unrevealed rooms in every corner; for what the universe is where the call contacts watchers, and the kingdom the same is named similar a cell of the voiced echo rejoices.

429. The eagle sweeps thine prayers, faith of the dove kisses you wisdom, saved attained doth sermoned eulogies expressed assured eagers persistence swooped respect.

430. Enchantment brightens the sun above thine head and moon below thine feet, and equal prestige comforts the brokenhearted legitimizes the emotionless plead.

431. A footstep a day is a jump per hour, but by a minute leapt truces enhance glorious prudence exercised work believed motivation dicated eternal.

432. Once you polish the teeth of the bridge, captains of ships will rank you assignments maximizing positions to excel you esclated ranks.

433. Therefore the advancement today of outsmarting indiscretion is outstepping misperception orchestrating arrangements brightened intention tomorrow.

434. Brag about the shoes, but if gossip shows the footwear is flat a central thought stumps. pointless and the inessential unfriendliness of bare feet stubbed aggravate splinters from spit.

435. Deliverances of inequities captivate caution, foreshadowed leaves delegate kings.

436. A rodded-line slung shalt lift cities, but the sword who handles the nations hammers and emissions the massive collaboration retrieval discovers initial duty, smashing self-controlled admission in subordinary palaces and inveighing irreplaceable salute salvation is commanded tenacity inevitable.

437. A weightless purpose coincides overweighted case and compulsions undamages conventionalism.

438. The provocation Philosophy of scourge, scorn, scold, brash, iffy and hasty resent debugs the spinning wheeling malaise; however, the account fated by a resolver grabs hold of the frenzy.

439. Food and hands are fun of the baker, that the chief creator as us usual and themselves among I use, populate cooked feelings that enrich wildernesses unfound, and treats sermon much ceremonies lunched, kingdoms snacked, and heavens sculpt columns of dinned summits.

440. Learn from a candle of lucid knowledge, gather skills from smokable brightness, develop hope coped dragged through the watchful grabbed stars of devotion surrounding discipline and concerns controlled pessimism dismissed harken brief relief.

441. Typical hypocrites virtue cynicism, but hypocritical sin of habitual forfeit disqualifies stability; however- otherwise, a

pernicious coinciding procedure prunes limited thickness of disillusion. Preservation provokes shinner obstacles, through inclined tendencies of self-importance incorporates obstinate admiration brightens volunteering edgy dissimilarity for bringing ingenious reposed reproof clashes among being themselves.

442. Wither the newspaper is harder held in your left hand and book you appreciate is featured in your easy right, the pen of modesty mediates the life-written predestined phenomenon of its master; the ambassador self-introduces survival to be as the selective material outmanning tailgating arguments un-neutral their chased criticism, doing uncooperative disfavor of dissolving the disparagement from those underestimated separated aside the churlish anarchists against those that outclass them.

443. A cup of coffee banks neither or no free cream better buttered charismatic care to be surcharged a discount of relinquished enjoyment, since the time it was composited; unlike dismal lighten overbearingness inactive depiction unbelievable to control; if caffeine strains the product then he who pours the first round a prophet claims shall bear nothing candid supplies bunched in a piled collected a lot, thenceforth this thereof will be bankrupt round him is the erroneous wicked devaluing several subversive faults severe.

444. Hooks rain horns ships during the almighty storm, but a thunderous shoves censured tempest of elation handling rudiments vessels wailing walls, leading gargantuan firmaments wings mark their slid timbers streaked. Remind yourself to disavow the collapsing hedges of the temples to

be subconsciously subdued closed toward confronted the affronted insecure disputed aperatures shut, bickering of begrudged proclivity operated spanks insolence inside the inexplicit transfused message translated.

445. There is a system of faith in the imbuing apparatus of finer evidence behind our backs unseen, the prevalent footprints left below and kissed groomed in the land of your sandals. The blood and sweat that is engraved tumultuously scores surmounted discord scourged scolders in limitless days here between indifference are impotent naked smiles and irremissible replicas dismiss tactful disloyalty yields recipient visited families sermoned in the showcase. Unless recognition isn't compromised smog of obfuscation and stereotyped discombobulation discrepancies chop logs of wood recorded at pinpointed uncertainty estimated, that will quit lugging incandescent happiness axes of arrows overhead whip.

446. Perhaps a supposable boasted tongue of the mouth suppers malnourished speech and rhetorical emphasis feelings wheezing retracted restriction that disappoints fierce policy; it misjudges the outlooked substandard manners, this reckoning preponderates much substantiated recognition only entitled for most applied authority.

447. Accounted resolution listens cohered discussions, but those that deride the distrusted of the room periodic abandonment leaves the wilderness of the fields, disposing poised the principal pragmatist's conviction disjoined contrasted implausible principle consideration, where

lectures itemize pointless repetition and preferences of specific variances constitute acquaintances.

448. A servant's difficult simplistic appearance smiles smirked sounder and brings obedient ridged audiences forcefully tighter, intricate competition integrates intent countryside noblemen claim.

449. Your heart calls justice of action, your thoughts judge adapted performance, but your soul deploys instinct dreaded of peace, and quality connecting detaile decided detains retention of disarrayed order reset opportunity undivided plausibly possible.

450. Neither never mountains vague of blood brushed swept in my veins shalt sweep flawed vain or vanity filled paint below the canyon, or above the valley to brighten masterpieces polished dubious fantasies famous demeanors generally hither boastful buckets of portrayed images credited excitement exceedingly robusts.

451. Tear the disloyal wound of the peg and a fatal reed will recede rebuked help and heed the distressed traveler upright curves of toned shape mode mad and smite firm unbent opposed crooked repressed. And the bridge of the stilts do not tatter, shake, crack, flea cotton, reproach crept a transgressive pest or reap sowed woes interwoven; its passion would't flip, flatten or flop but flapped vines swept wept branches unexposed distraught fraught agony to splinter the pipes. Thou of this flute creaked snapped boards of this receiveth orphaned ark custodian a parent, and apparent

shall cometh harken roundly brought extolled the girth of griped-grief gripped triumphant.

452. Lead as felt fallen, your thoughts noncore weren't dragged from tagged behind, but silence rose brags quietly rump, cunningly whispered from behind. Return back that setting you've been unLOVEd levitated brought back recovered; throughly follow remembered as someone pinched you tapped awoken, being charged first in control.

453. So you have a pebble, that's fine because it's better than the timeless disvalued property of presented sand. Such substance is rare at best distinguishable one it is purposeful. Bury it and then dig for art thou uncovered the hollow shell which shall and should uncover invested LOVE in that unreported tooth softspoken protection private. Once you blow troubles of terrific gospels spinning breaths of spiraling stress tirelessly invoked vocal stealth, serenity gives you back a brick, next you obtain a home, but further along the expedition the camp of your promises pack a tent of the hunted foundations you indented on a stone; this forest is your possession, then the objective of the posession slung fishes a cloud inclusive drenched incisions feistier.

454. The wing of the ocean hooks a friend; the pal that swims peckers cordial welcomes honores an invite acquaintance, unquestioned by convinced bait of generosity despite tendencies of the the repudiation steeps of huffy officers deeply irate the irritant unapologetic mistreatment staggering steep step cagey of ownership your gorgeous valleys rain. Offsprings of praises are eventually retrieved, while you urge to ascend your brow above the waters, the

Cory Morr

rest of nature will assign assistants of them according to the travelers abidded aside to assist assets whose ready to enormously fortify the confronted turmoil influences a float. Neither wrath of doom or upon disfavored plundered shalt collapse the star between a chariot of wolves and our determination which we apart climb the cliffs us lions are heading toward among expedient voyages.

455. Sarcastic products diffused incompetence alongside accompanying bargains of kosher obnoxious torment, are impossible monotonous collusions never unwilling hilarious compliments co-assisting neutral subsequences of relieved offenses; the unscrupulous mighty rivers of the sun forge uprise of the uppermost piety prudence the pure preceviers engenders. This interacted council harks miracles of the most technical undermining emotional excavation extravagance which irrecoverable candlesticks on top hills plot and their holders torching benches of juries fingers untaken folly to recoil the accounts that nobody foils my lips of mine and can eventually drudge the burnt platitude begrudged distributed persistence permises permissions constant qualification that judicial aspiration harps my lamps.

456. Surrogate exhilaration is overwhelming gladness, but overhauling loyalty conforms dignity.

457. The sick refute benign help, nowhere worthless pleasances choses saved useful consolation constitues challenged chaos underminded pacification.

458. A parent miscarries guilty purity as pleasure, for the innocents pitied price of pride overpaid humbleness

disowned then afterwards approached are throughful establishments divorced epitome themselves.

459. I brainstorm a stretched resolution of sunlight a gentle blanket covers of my Foundation of the lands of my face and which no pillers will examplify my countanance.

460. Invoked insanity inside the intellect of unconsidered insight miscounts steriol commodity.

461. The soup of the day is the Philanthropy from beginning to end sandwiched below the barrel to the top of the kitchen counter station and last the feasting table.

462. The cake of the reward and the pie of the paramount promotion benefits the identical anonymous server benevolent.

463. The discipline of the principle and the obedience of the obeyer is the principal obligator obscene only skillful conscienceness thoughtful.

464. Ageless radiances floods special care swam procuration sailors demarcate unbothered underhands the imbalance of ageless vanity entrusted eternal history.

465. Popularity below the headache of the mind crowds adequate esteemed fortitude above the belt, which stern sentiment overturns swizzled stomachs sickens astute self-disciplin.

466. Around every challenge opposed epidemics of obstacles surround ingenuity promoted enervates restless hypocrisy engineering dicated realiability.

467. Recipes of proficient efficiency and commitments commands resuscitated effort sufficed paths baking additional accredited receipts.

468. Oblation is intrepid imprecision in an ocean of epitome hallelujah harked heard harold excited glory eliminated ubiquitious urgency is repaid concentration of rapid focus.

469. You open a dresser of clothes, but the money in the pocket pulled will undress the heartless.

470. Voices and hymns will seed the unseen sounds sermoned sent, but silences muffled stumbled a stump stomps the scowlers.

471. A butterfly contrains enriched harmony unrestraint to enable the essence of the dove, which an eagle inspires the eager-edged saint.

472. Stories you elaborate and chronicles recorded stab us sensational pins and needles.

473. We seek to gain us an audience of peace for we ourselves are pieces of incredible crowded balance.

474. You wear a multiplicity of the sun on your head, entire authority on top is enticed wholesome by a system of order, which wares worrisome lamentation that unsound

impulsions tilt, until that belt of these tighter dilemmas dislodge the grunted fickle befallen.

475. You can adjoin along-by-aside me, for myself, a belonging demeanor of decision chosen between you and I, however positioned altogether we articulate those and themselves that often we refuse purposeless and pointless ambition to sober heavier drunk assessments of accessible normality is real intent which infiltrates moral composition of impervious compliance maneuvering uprightness.

476. I juggle discombobulated ridged jealously in a jiffy where sublime admiration jingles.

477. Once the thoughts and feelings of retrospection swim, run, and fly warriors of animals the kingdom doors of simplicity unlock, then accross deadbolts of redesigned ingenuity compensation serenity.

478. Priority management of from the propriety serviced breakfast, lunch, and dinner is a quality indifferenced arguments of a fattening dessert are contagious to reinforced fruited deity presided.

479. Devise diverse desire of bringing every and each brought circumstance made accounted, your internal especially external obtrusion of character will be controverted dismissal of their dependence, being counted their measures until trust ensures reliability is physically lured for us to us as we should so innoculated subconscious reinvigoration

aspired esteemed and therefore oblation toward ourselves the peaceful plan altogether.

480. You have concluded to cancel discontinuation consumption of your meal, however the last bite of those trays inadvertently unfastened disappoint remorseful mourning despaired overlong a dragged strenuous effort valiantly tenacious, disowning the tedious occupation disorder you oppose purchasing, but the exaggerated catch of surprises are standing at the door with an entree of famished employment, justifying the room around the straw you're then unlocks them the best part sipped approval preserved; advancement decoded turns the keyed complimentary special product of adopted anonimity adapts recruited a featured favored item inside the concession beverage served saved an aptitude appetite enriched entailing detail dubbed debtless.

481. Items of excuses drown in pool of suffocation and a crater of Asphyxiation facilitate recommended exceptional options of opinion to outsmart the lifeless faculty overworked enslaved frailty dissolved hopeless.

482. I am intoxicated undamaged in a bottle of unbiased enthusiasm unimagined, from which therefrom consequence melts an unapologetic icicle that a denseless society asleep soulless refuged refuted habituates guzzled shivers hibernated.

483. Mortified habits of thine humor that hath thee unashamed harbors discovers counterpart coinciding mates on a softhearted delicate softspoken delicate platform.

484. Overestimated idiocy galvanizes trash ouside windows and gusts of touched conditions simplify stupendous currents, privileged door bells overpower lodged grace and loaded slept faith overturns slacked laziness leaped relaxation that self-lead headaches unclasped a snowy sack handy for fixing waves of unwaken wacked wimps wanted.

485. Descended independence deviates deviance devoted to decided instinct durable.

486. Steam stagnation imbued ahead to stab stubborn emphasis of misinformed read illed sickeness unbiased reported messages debunked themselves corresponded poignant.

487. Store bites of broken vivid memory eager talent avid among valid policy affirms unstripped sensational prided politeness policed.

488. Whole subjects have their days, entire categories own their nights, but indefinite roles oncoming our way on the road and along the paths among the trails characterize a setting belonging granted assurances alongside resolved trials.

489. Ideas intercept internalized identity as an allegorical metaphor intersection of checked insightfulness intercrosses undiscovered grand openings to exercise.

490. Dwelling marks axed optimism obtains a shovel that hands scoops of gorges, and then for art thou the gullies are unconcealed, my head strings ropes of rung architecture,

my feet signs the lease of the foundation, a tenant lent a compass neither misdirects obscure obstruction between retrospected subdivided---subversion which coincides sentimental heritages summoned those entities.

491. A twitch itched bothersome unamused plucks entices fidged snitches; inhibited cracks of rude cruelty creeped shattered chunks of the ice splatter instead hummed of humor cherry pulled habitual dictations of demarcations practiced.

492. There is an animal on every aisle of the supermarket, 2 between each other side of much food products shelved stretched row by line and extended column through the supplies file. The vessel of the store scrounging the domed prison of its belly gurgles a corporate wilderness. Alter the feelings felt in the the fields of the recipe, churlish taste unsound reproaches stale transgressed vintages outdated unasked expirations original carryout lists of orders collected unmask. Conscience ancestors swore scrapped extinction vanished their disappeared conditioned distended cradled candles warn huge memorabilia had un-forsaken.

493. Contaminate confinement clawed refinement reclines the flex expelled funky extinguished exhaustion, which embeds permanent noncompliant strains stretched chastened; the outwitted provoked troublesome diversion contrasting integrated spoilage miscarry absurd gimmicks orchestrated from the asinine unearthly cretins.

494. Once support around the shopping cart is avowed plentiful, nourished dinner time catches chewed lands

caved on courses while chaperoned chapels of dishes, bowls, and cutting utensils perch fine platters of edible livestock nonperishable; affirmed self-expressed emotion exhibits discontinued settings edited features perpetuate seated series of settled surprises, that which often connect across this about them and thereof 1 of each X container of item will feed the starvation breed amended countrysides.

495. Banquets shalt nourish wholesome antiques feasts embarrassed anticipate impish antiquated priested beasts are unprecedented cowards heath harkened self-preserved exposure steadfast municipal chairmen thirst and the hungry spake healthier, punishing viewpoint prospection overstuffed abundances; their array continents captive outsell architecture which who typical merchant refrigerate farmlands exhausted habitual habitances.

496. A facetious remark gladdens glory, while which glorified compliments grunt gestured harmony, but serenity nonstop exponential unpaid compensates pricelessness.

497. Embark and sing melodies marked wings of flapped wind the echoed voices of chilling spuds spring encourage bravery of from courage rung, also assist unto accompanying tasked action rung performed nods of greets of acquainted talents tout impression uniqueness shrivels fidgidy inappropriate follies. Recommendation impeccable as advised options of its suggestion surrogates replies.

498. The indisputable useless are thoughtlessly inconceivable, mishandling the truth seen, heard and undecided; however, the wholehearted brainstormers extend the validity watched,

listened, and felt rightful ending unique fineness mantling organic vindication. Conflicts of infringements outbalance disinterested confrontations, which the remission remainder reminds us of the slips fathoming puddles of the offenses most mopes detest mopping their unmistaken trailing tears of slurs from repudiation slumps. Allow condonation of a pillow afflicting rectifying feathers for mastering and fathering affiliated escaped light laughable; afterwards soon, hardheaded strokes of rocky subconscious material professes exhausted distraction immunity that shalt intercede friendship-matured-partnerships, bridging their delicate softness spiked a kiss and gentle heeded LOVE centralizes the sharper points deepened staged rival retreated.

499. Often onward timelessly for anyhow and therefore usually awhile an insightful glance of the moon and sun's eyes wears a bikini of spiritual surveillance. When the obtained metaphysical goggles active concessions of envy divorcing epitome of traumatized watchful focus the tormenting spiral staircase deescalated the tumbling today by the base and trembles captivates triumphant tribulation at the core tomorrow; there is no larger unread yesterday unsound harder as incomparable forthcoming smaller and stronger conducive accomplishments covered better previously. Codes of superficial surreal substandard authority misconduct disappears rugged frustrations, coughing unneutralized concentration conforming to an applicable forefront dilapidation dismantled. Be insane of righteous infamy, bothering yet otherwise insecure scrutiny forgetting misbegotten pansies, but outstandingly lead loads of fantastic modernized royal justice dedication such moral snugged

compulsion employable that this convection conversed are stupendous to sin obiviated that particular frenzy. A CD'S erased content deletes its imminent disharmony and dissociates paranoia rendering its indecision criteria blanked irretrievable upon directorial material; licensed unworn updates advances durable trust from reshaped space unconcealed. The constituted subject matter circumventing the coincided character issue disposes the operator programing a cleaner climax establishement institution element which technicality outplays traditionalism. A defragmented heritage displaces unacquainted generations disestablishing faculties of contageious slower-sped symptoms safe mode self-labels. The condition of the files typically backed-up expendable redundancies store among themselves along and as once beside anyone ourselves recycle the trash bin obsolete; furthermore nevertheless, the trash bin of irrecoverable software protect safely reduplicated interminable instinct to undo being duped persuasions lost and stolen data of groups marked subversive disassociations. Those self-helped feelings cross exceptionalism, opposing irreversible referral hardware orphaned. Perhaps, I should change the destructible treatment of my invincible attitude, until the medium-core of my uncorrupted-upon-imbalanced essence is dermined extraordinary.

"500." Once is said, and needless indirect instructions are unquestionably further Quiet unquit stipulation. Demands of commenced reformation is further through---thorough requirements of actions that those assessment features a series of unopposed applications for programed pragmatism handed---provided practical instruments incorporated relieved hardship of assignment and a roof over of my head is now where my feet laid a pillar upon me and my nations foreign towers floors sweps of dust slide dirt of burnt ash off taken away and hidden below underneath; seditious sorrow that is sacred character finishes; nevertheless, refurbished immaculate sleeplessly exhausted toward being evermore the forceful star of vehement. This inseparable resolution reborn is classic, a reminiscence enriched diligence so personified its finest horizon of goals and manageable skills suffuse propagated worth of ubiquitous fortunate reborn

"R<3E<3S<3U<3R<3R<3E<3C<3T<3I<3O<3N!"

CARE AND HONOR
MANAGEMENT

.Conformity of a phenomanon mesmerizes the mesmerizes the mischievious basics.

.Appropriate quitness applies an application of congestive resilance.

.Rope your atrocity hammered from every tied corner simply intrucive.

.Entice rain showers of sprinkled reason which further rises enabled dedication.

.Acknowledge cyncism is an epidemic drowning the wheel of hypocrisy.

.Nothing negated toward an avid decision abandons a regreted option.

.Discontent admitted impounds discretionary partnerships disconnected.

.Hope spins cycles of righteous episodes bringing rejoiced trust chattered.

.Open a meaner-demeanor elongated as often the confidence rumbles.

.Neutral pacification is the passive indicator which points spectacular deals.

.Occupy obligation to your condition of an afraid horse, but the creepy rider controls it.

.Retribution adminstered designs a suspected changed solutions.

.Manipulation is a squeezed sponge while bacterial neighbores the mindset.

.Available action accomplished assessses around how major or minor the degree zipper grabs.

.Noble ethics is anyone's world throughout a single page of foundation.

.Accounts of sounded music contrive dealt instict in a discovered file of collapsing care.

.Groups of services are the discontinued treatment divested in a breakfast bowl of assignments.

.Entitlements beings narrow as the clot of possession bags stretched miles.

.Muffled begging of a participator captures the gabbled crops clapped miles.

.Enlist shared wisdom shaved below the brusstles sharp power mellows.

.Nifty trends from obsessive value is the teamwork pattern of tradition.

.Talent is hosted by only the self-created technition unscripted.

Cory Morr from Naples, Florida, is a successful self-publishing book author who previously wrote the initial epic and fantasy sci-fi novel The Blue Sphere in 2013 and does it again after publishing his second novel years later.

Printed in the United States
By Bookmasters